LEADER'S GUIDE

From the Moving Toward Maturity Series

Barry St. Clair

Moving Toward Maturity Series
  Getting Started
  Following Jesus (Book 1)
  Spending Time Alone with God (Book 2)
  Making Jesus Lord (Book 3)
  Giving Away Your Faith (Book 4)
  Influencing Your World (Book 5)
  Moving Toward Maturity Series Leader's Guide
  Spending Time Alone with God Notebook

Produced by REACH OUT YOUTH SOLUTIONS
                            3961 Holcomb Bridge Road
                            Suite 201
                            Norcross, GA 30092

All Bible quotations, unless otherwise indicated, are from the Holy Bible, New International Version.

©1973, 1978, 1984, International Bible Society. Used by permission of Zondervan Bible Publishers. Other quotations are from the King James Version (KJV).

ISBN: 1-931617-13-9

1 2 3 4 5 6 7 8 9 10 Printing/Year 10 09 08 07 06 05 04 03 02 01

The usage of the pronouns "his/he/him" has been used throughout this book for the sake of continuity and uniformity. The reader should assume these references refer to both male and female.

THE BIG PICTURE

FOLLOWING JESUS

Leader's Guide prepared by
Barry St. Clair and Juanita Wright Potter

Leading Your Discipleship Group

Moving Toward Maturity is a five-part discipleship training series for young people. It is designed to help them become independently dependent on Jesus Christ and then teach others to do the same. This series has four main purposes:

1. To encourage students to passionately pursue Jesus Christ.
2. To help young people develop strong, Christ-like character.
3. To train young people in the "how to's" of Christian living.
4. To move young people from the point of getting to know Jesus Christ to the point of offering Him to others.

Following Jesus, the first book in the series, introduces students to the basics of discipleship: becoming God's child, developing a relationship with Jesus Christ, discovering God's purposes, love and will, learning to study the Bible and pray, putting God first. It contains 10 Bible studies, 10 memory verse cards, and a "Bible Response" sheet for use in a daily study of 1 John (see session 7).

The other four study books in the series and related materials are described on the outside back cover of this Leader's Guide.

IMPORTANT NOTE: This Leader's Guide contains vital instructions, hints, and direction to help you lead your group most effectively. **We have placed this important information in only one place in the Leader's Guide, pages 6-11 in the *Following Jesus* section of the Leader's Guide.** Each time you begin a new book, review thoroughly the "Leading Your Discipleship Group" material. By doing so, you will sharpen your own leadership abilities. Through God's Spirit and your investment, students' lives will change.

SCRIPTURE MEMORY NOTE: Each Moving Toward Maturity book contains Bible memory verses that students memorize each week. These verses are found on the last page of each book. Since students tend to have trouble memorizing verses, your encouragement will help them succeed. The design of these books does not allow us to provide removable Scripture memory cards. Help by giving them ten small blank cards with a rubber band. Each week, when you make the assignments, have them write out the verse for the week on the card. Encourage them to carry the verses with them to review during the week. Keep extra cards in case they lose them. Helping your students succeed in memorizing Scripture is one of the greatest gifts you can give them!

Call to Commitment

Commitment is the key to a successful group study of *Following Jesus*. So limit the group to those young people who will commit themselves to study the book and the Bible on their own and will faithfully take part in every group meeting. This group of committed young people and their leader is called a Discipleship Group. (Turn to page 11 in *Following Jesus* and read the commitments required of each person.)

By making and keeping these commitments, each Discipleship Group member will:
1. Learn to passionately pursue Jesus Christ.
2. Develop personal discipline in Bible study, prayer, witnessing, establishing and following God's priorities, and seeking and obeying God's will.
3. Experience the rich fellowship and love of a committed, caring Christian community.

The young people and leaders who commit themselves to this discipleship training will move toward Christ's goal for the church: "His gifts were made that Christians might be properly equipped for their service, that the whole body might be built up until the time comes when, in the unity of common faith and common knowledge of the Son of God, we arrive at real maturity – that measure of development which is meant by 'the fullness of Christ'" (Eph. 4:12-13).*

You, the Leader

Being a leader of a Discipleship Group will require more time and personal involvement than most activities, Bible studies, or Sunday School classes you may have taught in the past. As a member of the group (not just its leader) you should take part in all the commitments, activities, and assignments of the Discipleship Group. To get started, here are some things you will need to do.

1. Get familiar with the Moving Toward Maturity series (see back cover) and your role as a Discipleship Group leader. Besides the introduction of this Leader's Guide, two other resources by Barry St. Clair can prepare you for your role: *Jesus-Focused Youth Ministry* and *Building Leaders for Jesus-Focused Youth Ministry*. Both are available from Reach Out Youth Solutions.

2. Read through *Following Jesus* and this Leader's Guide. As you

---

*Quoted from *The New Testament in Modern English*, by J.B. Phillips, published by the MacMillan Company. Used by permission.

read, ask God to reveal to you those young people who should be a part of this group. Ask Him to direct your steps as you organize and lead your Discipleship Group.

3. Recruit for Your Discipleship Group. Announce plans for the formation of your Discipleship Group to all of the appropriate groups of young people in your church. Explain what will be involved in meetings, assignments, etc. Read the commitment sheet (page 11, *Following Jesus*) that all group members will be expected to sign. Invite everyone who is interested to meet you at a specific time and place for an in-depth introduction (see Session 1, page 12). Before that meeting, speak privately with each student you believe should be part of the group and encourage him to join. Your group will be most effective with four to eight people, and should not exceed twelve. If more people are interested, form a second group.

4. Purchase all of the materials you will need well in advance of the first meeting. Each Discipleship Group member (including yourself) should have his own copy of *Following Jesus*. Students will value the book more if they pay for it. Collect the money when you hand them the book. Everyone who is leading a Discipleship Group should have his own copy of the Leader's Guide. Make sure every group member has his own Bible.

5. Decide the best time and place to meet. Have everyone bring their school and work schedules to the first meeting so you can decide as a group when and where to meet for the next ten sessions. If possible, plan to hold the meetings in your home or the home of one of the group members. Meeting in the informal atmosphere of a living room or around a dining room table will help people open up and join in the discussions.

6. Allow at least one hour for each meeting. Suggested time allotments for each part of the meeting are given in this Leader's Guide. A total of 60 minutes is suggested for the introductory meeting (session 1); 75 minutes are suggested for sessions 2-11. Since these are not instructional classes, but meetings designed to build relationships and share insights, they should be open-ended. If you finish a session in 75 minutes, fine. But you should have the freedom to meet for 90 minutes if necessary, but not longer.

7. Get the group together for a fun activity. Before or after session 1, plan a fun get-acquainted activity (softball game, bike hike, retreat, pizza party, picnic) for the students who are interested in the Discipleship Group. This will help them to relax and begin to build relationships.

Building Relationships

Your role in the Discipleship Group is that of leader, not teacher. By explaining that you and all members of the group are in the process of becoming more mature disciples of Christ, you will begin to establish yourself as one of the group rather than as the "instructor." But because you are more mature in years and in experience than the young people in your Discipleship Group, they will look to you for insight, guidance, and example. If they can see that you genuinely love God and that you care about them as individuals, they will more likely form solid, loving relationships with God, with you, and with one another.

1. Meet with each group member. Schedule an appointment with each member of your Discipleship Group during the first week or two. Get to know his needs, interests, concerns, and goals. Share those things about yourself as well. This will help you see one another as unique, important individuals with feelings and ideas. It will also result in more meaningful discussions during your group meetings.

2. Keep a notebook. In your notebook, write your observations about members of your Discipleship Group. Regularly pray for each one by name. Keep track of individual needs and achievements. If someone misses a session, contact him personally. Help him when he has trouble understanding something from Scripture. Talk with him if he breaks his commitments. Call on him for his opinions during meetings. Build him up so he will be valued and appreciated by the group.

Also use this notebook for writing your plans/outline of each session, your evaluation of each session, and what you plan to do to improve as a leader.

3. Keep your pastor and church informed. While you're building relationships in your Discipleship Group, build relationships within the church as well. Keep your pastor informed as to what is happening in your group. Encourage group members to get more involved in the youth ministry and to strengthen their relationships with other believers – particularly other young people who are not a part of a Discipleship Group. Group members need to form strong relationships with one another, but they should avoid becoming a "clique."

4. Limit group membership. Because your Discipleship Group will build trust based on shared experiences, don't take in any new members once the group has been established. (If several new people are interested in joining, start a new Discipleship Group for them at a later date.) After completing the study of *Following Jesus*, challenge each person to renew his commitment and to continue with the group in the next book, *Spending Time Alone with God*.

Effective Meetings

The Discipleship Group's meetings are based on biblical principles of discipleship. Each session has at least one Group Life and one Individual Growth goal. It's important that you work toward accomplishing both each week.

1. Be prepared. Begin your preparation for each session at least five days in advance. Do the Bible study in *Following Jesus*, answering the questions for yourself, not as you think the students might answer. Then skim through the Leader's Guide suggestions to see if there is anything you need to do right away. Later in the week (one or two days before the meeting) finalize your preparation: Review the *Following Jesus* material and study the Leader's Guide suggestions, adapting activities according to the particular needs of your group.

2. Start on time. Since Discipleship Group meetings can last up to 90 minutes, ask everyone to come on time, or even a few minutes early. (Those who arrive early can use the time to get to know each other better or review Bible memory verses.)

3. Help students keep their commitments. Students are to complete their assignments in *Following Jesus* before each session so the meeting can be devoted to building on what the students are learning on their own. For that reason, the "Exploring God's Word" section of each session does not contain a verbatim review of the Bible study material in *Following Jesus*. Instead, students are given an opportunity to quickly look over the Bible study content and their written responses. Then the discussion that follows builds on and reinforces what students have learned during the week prior to the meeting.

Be sensitive to group members who may lack self-discipline and need extra encouragement and motivation to keep their commitments. Be positive. Recall how Christ loved, encouraged, and disciplined the early disciples; then follow His example in helping His new disciples along. If someone is struggling, meet with him individually and/or with other group members to help him prepare.

4. Develop skill in leading discussions. Initially you will probably have to guide discussions by asking a question, getting a response, then asking another question. After several sessions this question/answer time will develop into group conversations as members get to know one another better. The sharing of insights from individual Bible study will cause the Scripture to have a greater impact in each person's life. As group members become more comfortable in speaking with one another about their lives in Christ, they will also be more at ease in speaking to others outside the group. Here's how to keep your Discipleship Group discussions on track so each member can contribute and learn during each session:

- State questions clearly and concisely. You're more likely to get specific answers if you ask specific questions.

- After you ask a question, allow time for the group to think. Don't be afraid of short periods of silence. And don't jump in with your own answers or opinions. Don't make a contribution to the discussion that someone else in the group can make.

- Respect each person's comments. Encourage each one to say what he thinks, not just what he thinks he should say. Ask additional questions to help him amplify his thoughts and move from ideas to applications.

- Stay close to Scripture. The Bible is the authority for this study and for your group discussions. Encourage group members to base their comments on biblical principles.

- Challenge trite or superficial answers. Don't let group members get away with simply rattling off a cliché or a Bible verse. Ask them to explain what they mean or give an illustration.

- Ask review questions when appropriate to help the group think through things they've learned up to that point. Use this time for students to raise previously-discussed issues with which they're still having problems.

- If some members answer all the questions, begin addressing your questions to others by name so that everyone may be heard. If a member continues to monopolize the discussions, you may want to talk with him privately after the meeting. Let him know you appreciate him and his contributions, but ask him to give others more opportunity to take part.

5. Evaluate each session. Within 24 hours of each meeting, evaluate how the session went and note the emerging needs of group members. The "After the Meeting" section of each session in this Leader's Guide can help you do this.

As you prepare to lead each meeting, pray that God will help you model the life of a true disciple. Be enthusiastic about growing spiritually, helping others grow, and sharing your faith with non-believers. Your spirit can be contagious.

If group meetings are enjoyable and helpful to each person in the Discipleship Group, he will not only grow in his relationship with Christ and the rest of the group, but will probably be eager to commit himself to the Discipleship Group again until all five books in the Moving Toward Maturity series have been completed.

I N T R O D U C T O R Y   S E S S I O N

Becoming a Discipleship Group

OVERVIEW

Key Concept   To benefit most from a group study of *Following Jesus*, we must commit ourselves to the disciplines of a Discipleship Group.

Goals   *Individual Growth:* To accept the responsibilities and commitments of the Discipleship Group.

Group Life: To establish a foundation for developing strong fellowship ties within the group.

BEFORE THE MEETING

1. Study pages 6-11 of this Leader's Guide for important background information.

2. In *Following Jesus*, study pages 1-11, and look over the Bible memory verses in the back of the book.

3. Call each person who said he would come to the first meeting. Remind him to bring his school and work schedules. Express your personal interest in him becoming a part of the Discipleship Group.

4. Based on your knowledge of the young people who are coming to this first meeting, make a note of each one's needs before the meeting. Ask God to help you present the challenge of discipleship in a fresh and exciting way that will motivate each person to study *Following Jesus* as a part of the Discipleship Group.

5. Gather materials for the meeting:
   • Bible
   • *Following Jesus* (one for each person)
   • Package of construction paper of various colors
   • Pencils
   • 3"x 5" cards
   • Memory verses

THE MEETING

BUILDING THE GROUP (20 minutes)

As each person arrives, ask him to write his name, address, phone number, and e-mail address on a 3" x 5" card. Then have him choose a sheet of construction paper and tear or fold it into a shape that symbolizes what he hopes God will do in his life as a result of being a part of this Discipleship Group. (Take part in this activity.)

Have everyone respond to each of the following questions before moving to the next question. (You go first.)

1. **What is your full name?**
2. **Where do you live?**
3. **What are you favorite activities?**
4. **Describe your symbol.**

FOCUSING ON LIFE (5 minutes)

Ask: **What can make belonging to a family a good experience?** (love, encouragement, sharing, etc.) Record responses.

EXPLORING THE CHALLENGE (20 minutes)

Read Ephesians 4:11-16, emphasizing how we as Christians can help each other grow and become mature in Christ.

Describe the Moving Toward Maturity series and the purpose of the Discipleship Group (page 6 of this Leader's Guide). Share your own enthusiasm about what this experience can do for all of you. Stress how disciplined commitment to God and to other group members is the key to success.

Give everyone a copy of *Following Jesus*. Collect the money for the book at this time. Review the contents and read the group disciplines (page 11). Discuss any questions students have about the commitments they are expected to make.

Briefly discuss the time (one and one-half hours per week with the group plus individual study time) and the number of weeks (10 more). Decide on a specific time and place to meet.

CONSIDERING THE CHOICE (15 minutes)

Review the positive characteristics of being a part of a family listed earlier. Ask the group to silently consider how those characteristics can apply to a Discipleship Group. Ask each person to write on his paper symbol the one group discipline in which he feels he will need the most encouragement and group support. Ask each one to share what he wrote. (If you share first, other group members will find it easier to share.)

Challenge the group to think and pray about making the commitment to a Discipleship Group. Encourage them to talk it over with their parents. Anyone who decides not to become a part of this particular 10-week Discipleship Group should let you know before the next meeting and return his unmarked copy of Following Jesus. Those who choose to join should come to the next meeting with all assignments in Session 1 completed. Encourage everyone to set aside a specific time each week to do the assignments for the next week (preferably at least five days in advance). This will give them several days to work on the memory verse and carry out any extra assignments that may be given in the Bible study.

Pray for each person by name and for his decision about joining this Discipleship Group. Thank God for what He is going to do in all of your lives as you commit yourselves to Him and to each other.

Assignments for Next Week: Be enthusiastic as you give the following assignments in your own words:
1. In Following Jesus, read pages 9-10, study and sign the "Personal Commitment" (page 11).

2. Complete Session 1.

3. Memorize 1 John 5:11.

4. Bring a Bible, a pen or pencil, and Following Jesus to every meeting. Before students leave this first meeting, try to talk with them individually. See if they have any questions or problems. Encourage them to join the group, and let them know you care about each of them and their concerns.

AFTER THE MEETING

1. Evaluate the meeting: Did each person become involved in sharing his ideas and feelings? How can you more effectively involve each person in next week's discussions? Review the "Effective Meetings," (pages 10-11 of this Leader's Guide.)

2. This week, and every week, begin preparing for the next session at least five days in advance. Complete the session in Following Jesus, and read through the Leader's Guide suggestions.

S E S S I O N   1

Are you Sure?

OVERVIEW

Key Concept Spiritual growth can begin when we are confident that God has received us as His children.

Memory Verse 1 John 5:11

Goals *Individual Growth:* To confirm and thank God for salvation made possible through Jesus Christ.

Group Life: To accept and affirm one another as important members of the group.

BEFORE THE MEETING

1. Pray for each group member by name and ask God to give you wisdom in guiding each one into a life of committed discipleship.

2. In *Following Jesus*, do Session 1, writing your personal answers to each question. In the margins jot down other observations you may want to share or discuss with the group.

3. Memorize 1 John 5:11.

4. Contact each person who attended last week's session. Answer his questions and remind him of the meeting time and place. If for some reason he has decided not to join this Discipleship Group, assure him of your continued love for him and the hope that he will be able to join a future group.

5. Make a list of the names, addresses, phone numbers, and e-mail addresses of all the group members (from the 3" x 5" cards filled out last week). Make a copy of the list for each person.

6. Gather materials for the meeting:
   • Bible
   • *Following Jesus*
   • List of group members' names, addresses, and e-mail addresses
   • Memory verses

THE MEETING

BUILDING THE GROUP (20 minutes)
Greet each person. Make him feel at home. Welcome him as an important part of this Discipleship Group. Have everyone turn to the "Personal Commitment" sheet (page 11, *Following Jesus*). Read it together. Ask anyone who hasn't already done so to sign his sheet. (Be sure to sign yours too!) Then, as a symbol of mutual commitment and support, have everyone sign everyone else's commitment sheet.

Ask each person to say one word that describes how he feels about committing himself to the Discipleship Group for ten weeks (fear, excitement, uncertainty, etc.). Briefly discuss how any negative emotions can be overcome. Ask volunteers to offer short prayers about the emotions expressed and ask God to give everyone a vision for what He wants to do in your lives during the next nine weeks.

Enthusiastically assure the group of your availability and desire to help each one successfully complete this discipleship study.

FOCUSING ON LIFE (10 minutes)
Discuss: **Have you ever belonged to a group (band, baseball team, school club, etc.) and doubted your acceptance by others in the group? If so, how did you feel? How was your contribution to the group affected? How did your doubts cause you to react to others in the group?**

Explain that we can have these same feelings and reactions toward God and other Christians if we have doubts about our salvation. Share an example of this from your own experience or ask volunteers to give examples.

EXPLORING GOD'S WORD (35 minutes)
[NOTE: Each week this section is based on the work students have done in *Following Jesus*. The discussion questions are usually not identical to those in the book, but they draw from the same Scriptures and assignments. This technique helps students think through what they've studied rather than just parroting written answers.]
Allow time for everyone to review his written responses to Session 1 in *Following Jesus*. Then discuss:
1. What would you tell a person who says, "I feel fine just the way I am. Why should I become a Christian?" Response can be based on students' answers under "What is a Christian?"

2. In what ways did you find it hard to take any one of the five steps to salvation listed on pages 16-20? (For example, someone might say that he was too proud to admit his need of Christ until he faced a huge problem in his life that helped him see his need.)

3. How can you know if you're truly a Christian? Refer to the "How to Know if You're Really A Christian" section, page 22. In summary, answers should include:

John 2:3-6   True belief leads to obedience.

    3:14   Love for others develops.

    3:24; 4:13 Christ's Spirit lets you know that He is with you.

    4:15   Christians tell others about Christ.

    5:1   God promised that by believing in Christ we can be His children.

4. Of the five assurances given in 1 John, which one is most meaningful to you? Why? Give everyone an opportunity to answer. As a group, quote today's memory verse (1 John 5:11). Then offer sentence prayers of thanksgiving for the salvation God has given through His Son, Jesus Christ.

APPLYING GOD'S WORD (10 minutes)

Ask each person to write in response to Session 1: (1) One thing he will do this week to affirm his salvation. (Examples: Thank God every day that He remains true to His promises; tell someone else about what it means to him to be a Christian.) (2) One thing he will do this week to demonstrate his commitment to another member of the Discipleship Group. (Examples: Offer a ride to someone who may have a hard time finding a way to the next meeting; call someone during the week just to encourage him.)

Assignments for Next Week: As you give the following assignments, be positive. Let the young people know that you respect their desire and ability to be accountable.

1. Complete Session 2 in *Following Jesus*. Don't forget to memorize the Scripture verse.

2. Be prepared to share the results of what you do this week to affirm your salvation and to demonstrate your commitment to someone else in your Discipleship Group.

AFTER THE MEETING

1. Evaluate the meeting: Was the atmosphere relaxed? Did everyone feel free to take part? If not, jot down some possible causes and what you can do to improve the situation next week.

2. If anyone seemed uncertain about his salvation, be sure to get together with him and go through the Gospel. Offer him the opportunity to receive Christ.

The Great Discovery

OVERVIEW

Key Concept   Spiritual growth is based on knowing what God wants us to become and do.

Memory Verse   Philippians 1:6

Goals   *Individual Growth:* To discover God's purposes for His children and to begin taking the steps necessary to fulfill those purposes.

Group Life: To encourage one another in pursuing the goals of developing a close relationship with God; a mature, Christ-like character; and a life that represents Christ to the world.

BEFORE THE MEETING

1. Pray for all group members by name, asking God to assure each one of His presence and His love.

2. Complete Session 2 in *Following Jesus.* Remember, as a participant (not just the leader) in this Discipleship Group, take part in all group activities and discussions, but be careful not to dominate.

3. Memorize Philippians 1:6; review 1 John 5:11.

4. Gather materials for the meeting:
   - Bible
   - *Following Jesus*
   - Bible memory verses

THE MEETING

BUILDING THE GROUP (20 minutes)
Ask volunteers to share what they did this past week to (1) affirm their salvation and (2) demonstrate their love for someone in the Discipleship Group. Briefly discuss the results of what they did: How did they feel? How did others respond?

Ask the group to think about the behavior of people in general.

Discuss:

1. What are some of the life purposes people you know seem to have? (having a good time, making lots of money, getting by, etc.)

2. What evidences indicate that many people have no purpose for their lives? (boredom, unfinished projects, constantly changing plans, fear of the future, etc.)

3. How would having a significant purpose for living change the way they act?

FOCUSING ON LIFE (10 minutes)
Discuss:
1. Have you ever asked yourself, "Why am I here? Why was I born?"

2. What answers did you give before you were a Christian?

3. Have your answers changed at all since you studied this week's assignment?

4. Why do you think having a purpose in life is important?

EXPLORING GOD'S WORD (30 minutes)
Have students silently review their work on Session 2 in *Following Jesus*. Then discuss:
1. What are three purposes God has for our lives? (to establish a love relationship with God, to mature us in Christ, and to witness for Christ)

2. How would you describe a Christian's love relationship with God? (it begins with spiritual birth; it involves continual communication with God; etc.)

3. What role do we play in our relationship with God? *Refer to the sections on restoring and maintaining fellowship under "God's First Purpose", pages 25, for answers.* (We can break our fellowship with God by sinning; we can restore it by confessing our sins; we can maintain it by communicating with Him; etc.)

4. What are some characteristics of a "grown-up" or mature Christian? *Have students check Galatians 5:22-23 and Romans 12:2.* (He is loving, joyful, peaceful, patient, kind, etc.; he looks at things from God's point of view, not from the world's.)

5. Name at least three things you think God uses to help us become more like Christ. (His Spirit, His Word, and the events and people around us)

6. In 2 Corinthians 5:20 Paul describes Christians as "Christ's ambassadors." In other words, we are like diplomats sent from one country to another – we are sent from the kingdom of God to represent Him on earth. What are two ways we can fulfill our mission as ambassadors? *Refer students to the two main points under "God's Purpose #3."* (by our attitudes and actions toward others; by talking with others about Christ)

APPLYING GOD'S WORD (15 minutes)
Ask each group member to think about his life before he became a Christian and compare it with his life since he received Christ. Have each person (including yourself) share one example of how his life has changed and how that change could be a witness to others about Christ.

Have each one review silently what he wrote on page 24 to describe his purpose in life. Ask him to think of specific ways he can begin to act on his statement of purpose this coming week and to write them down in the book. If necessary, suggest some possibilities: how he spends his free time in the evenings or on weekends; how he responds to his parents when asked to do something; what he talks about when he is with friends; or the attitudes he has toward homework. Share your own purpose in life and how you plan to act on it this week. Then ask volunteers to do the same.

Ask two people to pray, asking that each group member will be able to move toward the goal of God's purpose for his life in the coming week.

Quote this week's memory verse (Philippians 1:6), then ask students to quote it with you. Review 1 John 5:11. Encourage group members to work in pairs between meetings to help each other with the memory verses.

Assignments for Next Week:
1. In *Following Jesus*, complete Session 3, "Lot's of Love."

2. Identify one or two other people in the group with whom you can work on memorizing Scripture.

AFTER THE MEETING

1. Evaluate the meeting: Did discussions stay away from clichés and abstractions, focusing on specific, practical, life-related ideas? If not, ask God to help you know when to probe deeper in next week's discussions.

2. If some group members are having difficulty keeping up with the assignments, call them during the week. Encourage them to stay with the group. Answer any questions they may have. Offer to help them work out a schedule. Meet with them to do the assignments, if necessary.

S E S S I O N 3

Lots of Love

OVERVIEW

Key Concept   Spiritual growth is rooted in an active love relationship with God.

Memory Verse   John 3:16

Goals   *Individual Growth:* To become aware of the character and quality of God's love and to consider ways to express love to God.

Group Life: To explore ways to express love to God and God's love to one another as a body of believers.

BEFORE THE MEETING

1. Pray for each member of the group and for the development of group unity.

2. In *Following Jesus*, complete Session 3, studying all Scripture passages mentioned.

3. Note breakdowns of human attempts at love which you may hear or read about during the week. Be ready to use one as an example to get the discussion started during the second activity of the meeting.

4. Gather materials for the meeting:
    • Bible
    • *Following Jesus*
    • Bible memory verses

THE MEETING

 BUILDING THE GROUP (20 minutes)
Ask the group to name and jot down the five characteristics of God's love outlined in Session 3 (unconditional, sacrificial, serving, forgiving, creative).

Ask them to think of specific instances, either their own or someone else's experience, where human love has broken down (broken friendships, quarrels with parents, divorce, runaways, etc.). As each member gives an example, have the group decide which of the five characteristics of God's love was the primary missing element in that particular instance.

Discuss how God's love differs from what usually passes for love in daily life. (Enliven the discussion by suggesting that they think of how advertisers use the promise of love as an end result of using their products.)

FOCUSING ON LIFE (10 minutes)
Discuss: **Have there been times when you have doubted God's love for you? Why? How can we get rid of such doubt?** (Focus on what God says.) Then say, **God does love us, but He wants us to love Him too. How can we express our love to God? Let's check it out.**

EXPLORING GOD'S WORD (30 minutes)
Give everyone a few minutes to review the contents and their written responses to Session 3 in *Following Jesus.*

Discuss the following issues, encouraging each person to contribute his thoughts and to jot down the ideas of other group members.

1. **If someone told you, "The way to love God is to go to church, read the Bible, and pray," what would you say?** (That's only the beginning, a small part, an outward expression of what it means to love God.)

2. **From what you know of Jesus' life on earth, what are some specific ways He expressed His love for God to God? to others?** (He took time to pray, rejected Satan's tempting offers, obeyed His Father even to death; fed the hungry, healed the sick, loved those whom others found unlovable.)

3. **How do Jesus' expressions of love to God and to others relate to the five characteristics of God's love outlined in today's session?** (They demonstrate God's kind of love.)

4. **What can you do to express your love for God with your heart? your soul? your mind? your body?** *Answers may be based on student's written responses to "Making It Personal."*

5. **How can your love for God be expressed by the way you treat your family? your friends? the guy who keeps annoying you in study hall? the teacher who is a little too hard for you?**

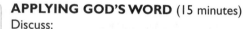

APPLYING GOD'S WORD (15 minutes)
Discuss:

1. How can we, as a group, express our love to God? *Suggest planning a special time of worship – praying and singing or reading the Bible – as a good beginning point and as a way to ask God for His answer to this question.* Once the group decides, then do it.

2. How might our relationships with one another express God's love? *Suggest that during the week they list ways they can make their relationships with each person in the group more serving, more forgiving, more creative, more sacrificial, and more unconditional.*

Encourage each group member to meet with at least one other member of the group for a time of sharing and praying before the next meeting. If he needs to mend or restore a strained or broken relationship with anyone in the group, he should meet with that person first. Strengthened relationships between individuals will help the whole Discipleship Group.

Quote today's memory verse (John 3:16) together. In response to God's sacrificial love for them, have several group members pray, thanking God for His love and asking for His guidance as they seek to express their love for Him this coming week.

Assignments for Next Week: Motivate students to do next week's assignments by saying, **Do you ever have trouble loving yourself or others? This week's session will help you learn to accept yourself and others by exercising God's kind of love.**
1. Complete Session 4. Write down any comments, questions, or pertinent thoughts. Memorize 1 John 3:23.

2. Get together with one person from the group during the week for prayer.

AFTER THE MEETING

1. Evaluate: Are two or three people dominating the discussions at each group meeting? If so, talk with them privately. Let them know you appreciate their contributions; but ask them to work with you in helping everyone take part.

2. If there is a person in the group with whom you need to mend or strengthen your relationship, set a time and place to meet with him.

S E S S I O N 4

Love To Spare

OVERVIEW

Key Concept   Spiritual growth involves learning to love ourselves and others with God's kind of love.

Memory Verse   I John 3:23

Goals   *Individual Growth:* To gain a new sense of self-worth and begin expressing love to those who seem especially unlovable.

                  Group Life: To become a source of acceptance, appreciation, and love for one another.

BEFORE THE MEETING

1. Pray that the relationships between individuals in your Discipleship Group will be strengthened during the coming weeks.

2. Complete Session 4 in *Following Jesus.*

3. Write one thing you like about each person in your Discipleship Group.

4. Gather materials for the meeting:
   • Bible
   • *Following Jesus*
   • Bible memory verses

THE MEETING

 **BUILDING THE GROUP** (20 minutes)
Ask volunteers to share their experiences of this past week as they talked and prayed with other group members. What did they learn about the other person? About themselves? Suggest that they all try to meet with each person at least once during the next six weeks.

Say: **Under "Loving Yourself" in Session 4, you were to make two lists: (1) things you don't like about yourself; (2) things you do like about yourself. How many of you had difficulty thinking of** things to put on that first list? **How many of you found it harder to come up with things to put on that second list?** **Since most of us find it much easier to think about things we like about ourselves, let's help each other add to our lists of likable things.** Ask each person in the group to name one thing he likes about each of the other group members – you begin. Let this be a fun, relaxed time.

FOCUSING ON LIFE (10 minutes)
Discuss:
1. What relationship is there between how you feel about yourself and how you feel about other people? *Have students make a list of things they don't like about other people and compare it with the list of things they don't like about themselves.*

2. How does this comparison relate to what Jesus said in Mark 12:31? (He did not simply command us to love our neighbors. He knew that was impossible if we don't love and value ourselves.)

EXPLORING GOD'S WORD (30 minutes)
Have each person review "Loving Others," Session 4. Then discuss:

1. Why is it important for Christians to love other people? *Refer to insights from 1 John 4:7-19 for the answers.* (God is a lover; He loved us first and His love is made complete by our love for others; God lives in us; we can have confidence on the day of judgment; love drives out fear; we can't love God and not love others; God has commanded it)

2. How can we begin to love other people when we don't feel like loving them? *Refer again to 1 John 4:7-19.* (By knowing that love comes from God we rely on God's love; because love comes from God; God gives us His Spirit who lives in us and fills us with God's love.)

3. What did Jesus say was the best way for the world to know that we are His disciples? *Refer to John 13:34-35.* (by our visible expressions of love for each other)

4. How can we stop talking about loving others and begin to actually do it? *Refer to the "Loving Others" section, page 40.* (Ask God for His love; believe that He has given it; do a good and loving deed for someone you find hard to love.)

APPLYING GOD'S WORD (15 minutes)
As a group, quote today's memory verse (1 John 3:23). Then ask each person to share his experience this past week in showing God's love to a

person he has found hard to love. (Refer to their response under "Making it Personal.") Ask if they realize that while they are trying to express love to others, that doesn't necessarily mean that others will love them in return.

Ask: **How can we help each other when we get frustrated, angry, or discouraged by the actions of others?** (Call each other and talk about it.)

Close the meeting in prayer, asking God to help each of you realize that you have love to spare because God's love has the power to transform not only your lives but the life of each person you deal with each day.

Assignments for Next Week: Give the following assignments in your own words and with enthusiasm:
1. Complete Session 5.

2. Review all memory verses and be prepared to recite them.

3. Read "The Guest Who Took Over" in the back of *Following Jesus,* **as assigned in Session 5.**

NOTE: Mention that beginning with Session 6, each person will need a notebook for writing responses to daily Bible reading assignments in 1 John. We suggest that you order the *Time Alone With God Notebook* from Reach Out Youth Solutions for each person in the group. This book will provide consistency. If you decide not to order the notebooks, group members may already have extra notebooks at home they can use. Students can reimburse you for the cost when you hand them out at next week's meeting.

AFTER THE MEETING

1. Evaluate: Was the atmosphere of the meeting relaxed and comfortable? If not, why not? The room itself could be the problem if it is too hot or cold, lacks a homey warmth, has poor lighting or uncomfortable chairs, or isn't protected from outside interruptions. Find ways to improve the room, or look for a better meeting place. If the problem lies in poor group dynamics, review the suggestions for effective meetings on pages 10-11 of this Leader's Guide.
2. If any group members seem to be on the fringe, either not being accepted fully by the others or just not taking part in the discussions and activities, pray specifically for them this week. If possible, get together with them before the next meeting to express your love for them and to encourage them to share their thoughts and ideas.

S E S S I O N   5

Alive in You!

OVERVIEW

Key Concept　　Spiritual growth is made possible by the transforming power of Jesus Christ living in us.

Memory Verse　　John 15:5

Goals　　*Individual Growth:* To discover what it means to "remain in Christ" and to identify and develop the characteristics of a life in Christ.

Group Life: To encourage development of the Spirit's fruit in group members' relationships with one another and with their families, classmates, and other Christians.

BEFORE THE MEETING

1. Pray for each member of your Discipleship Group by name. Ask that they will all develop an understanding that being Christ's disciples does not depend on their efforts, but on Christ who lives in them and will work through them.

2. In *Following Jesus,* complete Session 5; read "The Guest Who Took Over."

3. Review all Bible memory verses.

4. Consider specific ways you can express love, joy, peace, patience, kindness, goodness, gentleness, faithfulness, and self-control to each group member when you talk or meet with him this week.

5. Gather materials for the meeting:
   • Bible
   • *Following Jesus*
   • Bible memory verses
   • A houseplant
   • *Time Alone with God Notebook* (one for each group member)

THE MEETING

BUILDING THE GROUP (15 minutes)

Divide the group into pairs and have partners take turns reviewing Bible verses memorized so far. Encourage those who know their verses to help those who don't by meeting with them during the week for practice. Ask volunteers to share any benefits they have received so far from hiding God's Word in their hearts.

Since you're halfway through this discipleship study, take a few minutes to review the main points of the first four Bible studies. Ask:

1. How can we know we are truly Christians?
2. What are three purposes God has for our lives?
3. What are five characteristics of God's love?
4. Why is it important for Christians to love other people?

Ask each person to share at least one insight he has gained that has been especially important in his life. Ask for any questions, comments, problems, or suggestions about the Discipleship Group, things you have studied, or the group meetings.

During a time of prayer, reaffirm the commitment of the group to Christ and one another, asking for guidance and wisdom in dealing with any problems mentioned in the preceding discussion, and thanking God for the truths that have been learned so far.

FOCUSING ON LIFE (15 minutes)

Discuss "The Guest Who Took Over," page 90 in *Following Jesus*:

1. What do the different rooms described in the article represent in your life? *Refer members to their responses on page 45-46.*

2. What difference does it make to know that Christ is with you, not just when you are in church or when you pray or read the Bible, but all of the time? *Encourage group members to share how this knowledge makes them feel and the difference it makes or could make in their attitudes and actions.*

EXPLORING GOD'S WORD (30 minutes)

Allow a few minutes for each person to review the rest of his responses to the assignments in Session 5, *Following Jesus*. Then discuss:

1. What are some things you can do to allow Christ to have

consistent control of your life? (confess sins; humbly submit to Christ's control)

2. How does this compare with how we learned to restore and maintain our fellowship with God? *Refer to Session 2, pages 25-26.*

3. What image did Jesus use to describe our relationship with Him? *Refer to John 15:5* (vine and branches). To make this image more tangible, hold up a houseplant and remind the group of the interrelatedness of each part of a plant. Point out that there is no great effort expended by each branch to produce the leaves, flowers, or fruit that characterize the plant – they are simply the natural result of being a part of the plant. The fruit comes from the nature of the plant, not from the hard work of each branch.

4. How are our lives in Christ like branches on a plant? (The power and fruit of the Christian life come from the nature of God – if we stay with Him, we will grow and become like Him.)

5. How are our lives different from a plant's branches? (We have the freedom to abide in Him or to go our own way.)

Ask the following questions:

1. What does it mean to "remain in"? *After each person has read his written definition, try to summarize all contributions into one statement.*

2. What are the results of remaining in Christ and Christ remaining in us? *Refer to John 15:5-11.* (We will bear much fruit; our prayers will be answered; God will receive glory. Our obedience will result in experiencing His love for us and the joy that He gives.)

3. What does God do to produce more fruit in us? *Refer to John 15:2-3.* (He trims away the deadwood – sinful characteristics that keep us from bearing fruit; and He nurtures spiritual fruit.)

4. What basic tool does He use for trimming and nurturing? (His Word)

Go over the list of deadwood characteristics that Paul gives in Galatians 5:19-21 (see "Making It Personal," page 49, *Following Jesus*). Make sure the meanings of the words are clear to everyone. For example, "debauchery"

(NIV) or "lasciviousness" (KJV) more simply defined mean "lustfulness" or "immorality." Then discuss:

1. Why are these characteristics considered "deadwood" for a Christian? (Because God's goal for a Christian is to be like Christ, and those things are not part of His character.)

2. Which of these is most prominent among young people today?

3. How does "deadwood" express itself in each of our lives? *Have each person share one piece of deadwood he sees in his own life – you share first.*

4. How can we help each other trim the deadwood out of our lives? (Encourage one another; be accountable to one another.)

Say: **When God trims us, He doesn't leave gaping holes in our lives so we have stubby, ugly lives. Instead He heals and nurtures us to produce beautiful fruit.** Then discuss:
1. What words does Paul use to describe this "fruit-filled" life? Refer to Galatians 5:22-23. (love, joy, peace, patience, goodness, kindness, gentleness, faithfulness, and self-control)

2. How prominent are these characteristics among the people we know at school, work, church, and home?

3. What is likely to be the result of our developing these characteristics in our lives – being kind, gentle, patient, good, etc. – and expressing them in the world around us?

 APPLYING GOD'S WORD (15 minutes)
Say: **While it is true that allowing Christ to live out the fruit of the Spirit in us will present us with new challenges with people because we will act differently, having the fruit of the Spirit will also help us handle the normal frustrations we face in our daily lives better.**
Ask group members to look over the list of frustrations they wrote on pages 43-44 in *Following Jesus*, and to think of specific ways that the fruit of the Spirit will help them handle those frustrations. Give them time to write down any new ideas they have. Then ask volunteers to share one or more of their ideas. (Examples: expressing thanks instead of complaints to parents; showing self-control and patience with little brothers or sisters;

being faithful in responsibilities at school or work; being at peace about dating relationships; not constantly speculating or worrying; being faithful to friends through hard times; practicing self-control to overcome negative thoughts, actions, and habits.)

Go over the section "Giving Christ Control," pages 46-47. Then quote the memory verse (John 15:5) together. Follow this with a time of silent prayer during which each person asks God for guidance in the specific areas of life he is having trouble with right now. Close by leading a prayer of thanksgiving for God's consistent presence, control, and power in your lives.

Assignments for Next Week:
1. Complete Session 6.

2. Spend at least ten minutes each day in Bible study as explained at the end of Session 6. *If you bought* Time Alone With God Notebook *for students to use for this assignment, give them out and collect the money now.*

3. Bring your *Time Alone With God Notebook* to the rest of our meetings so you can share with the rest of us what God is teaching you in 1 John.

AFTER THE MEETING

1. Evaluate: Do you find yourself giving more answers to the questions than the students are? If so, perhaps you're not giving them enough time to collect their thoughts. If there is a silent moment after a question is asked, don't rush in with hints or answers. Give everyone a chance to think through what they want to say and let them say it. Remember, as a Discipleship Group leader, you guide the group toward discovering and sharing biblical insights for themselves. Though you should correct any wrong interpretations, you do not lecture.

2. Be alert for anyone who may need to talk with you alone. As assignments and specific life applications increase, some members may feel too pressured or have questions or problems they can't answer or solve by themselves.

S E S S I O N   6

God Says ...

OVERVIEW

Key Concept   Spiritual growth is nourished by getting into God's Word on a regular basis.

Memory Verse   Psalm 119:9

Goals   *Individual Growth:* To begin studying the Bible every day and apply what is studied to daily life.

                    Group Life: To encourage one another to study God's Word every day and to remind one another of what has been learned.

BEFORE THE MEETING

1. Pray that each person will make time to study the Bible each day this week and that God will speak to each one in a special way.

2. In *Following Jesus*, complete Session 6, including the special Bible studies in 1 John.

3. Think of things you have learned and things people have told you that have helped you develop the habit of studying the Bible. Be prepared to share these with the group at the meeting.

4. Talk with several group members during the week to encourage them in their study and to let them know you care about them.

5. Gather materials for the meeting:
   • Bible
   • *Following Jesus*
   • Fiber-tipped pens in various colors
   • Plain sheets of paper
   • *Time Alone With God Notebook* (containing your notes on 1 John)
   • Bible memory verses

THE MEETING

BUILDING THE GROUP (15 minutes)
Ask for reports on the ten minutes of daily Bible study as assigned at the end of Session 6 in *Following Jesus*. Ask: **Were you able to set a specific time? Did you find a quiet place where you could be alone? Were you able to concentrate? Did you find the "Bible Response Sheet" easy to use?** Let this be a time where group members share ways to overcome specific difficulties or problems in following through on the Bible study time. Give examples from your own experience.

Ask several people to share one important insight they have gained from their study of 1 John so far.

FOCUSING ON LIFE (15 minutes)
Referring to the beginning of Session 6, page 52, *Following Jesus*, ask:
1. What can we learn about Jesus' study of God's Word from His encounter with Satan, recorded in Matthew 4:1-10? (He knew Scripture and used it to resist temptation.)

2. What would most people's response have been to the offer of bread after 40 days without eating anything? (Thanks a lot! I'm starving!)

3. What would have been their response to being offered all the land within sight from the top of a mountain? (Wow!)

Say: Because Jesus knew God and His Word so well, He knew what to say to Satan. He was able to recognize that Satan was tempting Him. Studying the Bible can make us more aware of what is going on around us and give us the insight and wisdom needed to deal with real life in both the seen and unseen world.

EXPLORING GOD'S WORD (40 minutes)
Give everyone a few minutes to review his work on this week's Bible study. Then discuss:
1. Why is the Bible such an important source of help for us as we seek Christ's control of our lives? *Refer to "Counting on God's Word," page 53.* (It is inspired by God for teaching, correcting, training, and equipping; it is alive and can change attitudes, thoughts, spirits, and personalities; it is authoritative – tells us God's will; it is the truth – and the truth gives us freedom to truly live life at its fullest.)

2. What are some benefits we gain from studying and obeying God's Word? *Refer to "Discovering the Benefits of God's Word," page 55.* (Maturity, prosperity, wisdom, understanding, light, guidance, a clean life, God's love and companionship [friendship], faith, ability to obey God)

3. If all we have talked about so far is true, and it is, then knowing God's Word should be one of our top priorities in life. But how do we go about knowing the Word? *See "Experiencing the Benefit of God's Word," page 56.* (hear, read, study, memorize, meditate)

Talk about what "hearing" the Word means. Encourage group members to attend church services regularly, take notes on messages given by the pastor and other Bible teachers, and write specific insights and applications to their lives.

Discuss the difference between "reading" the Word and "studying" it. Though everyone in the Discipleship Group is studying a small portion of Scripture each day, encourage them to start reading whole chapters or books at one sitting to get an overview of God's Word.

Turn to the 1 John, Daily Bible Reading Assignments on page 96, *Following Jesus.* Select one of the first five passages listed and work through it together, answering: Who? What? When? Where? Why? What does it say? What does it mean? How does it apply to me? What am I going to do about it?

Ask if Session 6 has clarified the purpose of the Scripture memory they have been doing for the past five weeks. Have each person recite one of the verses, personalizing it by inserting his own name where there are pronouns or words like "the world" or "the man." (Example: "I am the Vine; Jane is the branch. If Jane remains in Me and I in her, Jane will bear much fruit; apart from Me Jane can do nothing," John 15:5.)

Give each person a sheet of paper and a pen. Then ask everyone to draw a picture which illustrates Psalm 1:1-3. Allow about five minutes. Have them display their work and then discuss how this simple exercise helped them dig deeper into the verses and apply what was said to their lives.

APPLYING GOD'S WORD (10 minutes)
Encourage each person to continue in the 10-minute daily study of 1 John as outlined on page 96. If someone is having trouble scheduling his time, offer to help him work out a schedule after the meeting. Say: **Remember, the purpose of studying God's Word is not just so we**

can all answer the questions at our weekly meetings. His Word is to become a part of who we are. We are to use it, speak it, rely on it, share it, and let it affect every area of our lives. For this to happen, we must develop the habit of thinking about God's Word in every situation. For example: When we're discouraged by grades or work, angry at someone, or nervous about telling someone about God, we should ask ourselves, "What would Jesus say or do in this situation? What specific Scripture passage gives a principle that applies to this situation?" By consciously reminding ourselves of Scripture, our minds will turn there first when we need guidance or encouragement. And God will bring to mind actual Scripture passages to guide us in many daily situations. To reinforce this, quote today's memory verse (Psalm 119:9) together.

Ask several volunteers to close in prayer; have them pray for perseverance in their study of God's Word.

Assignments for Next Week: Motivate group members to:
1. Complete Session 7.

2. Continue daily study of I John and begin a daily prayer time as explained at the end of Session 7.

Be available as students leave to help anyone who needs suggestions for scheduling a regular time for Bible study (get up a little earlier, cut out some TV watching, etc.).

AFTER THE MEETING

1. Evaluate: Did everyone participate freely in all of the meeting's activities? If some group members still seem to be on the edge of the group life, ask one or two of the more mature members to give them special support and companionship during the next weeks. Also, think of ways you can make them feel more a part of the group meetings (Ask them to read Scripture; call on them by name, etc.).

2. Are some of your group members finding daily Bible study and prayer to be more of a chore than a joy? Commitment, determination, and self-discipline are needed for developing a relationship with God. But Bible study and prayer should be experiences that are enjoyed – not rituals that are endured. Try to talk with each person during the next couple of weeks to help him through any problems he may be having in this area.

S E S S I O N   7

Talking with God

OVERVIEW

Key Concept   Spiritual growth is stimulated by communicating with God through daily prayer.

Memory Verse   John 16:24

Goals   *Individual Growth:* To explore the importance of prayer as a part of a disciple's life and to begin praying daily.

Group Life: To understand why prayer is an important part of loving and encouraging others and to begin praying for one another on a regular basis.

BEFORE THE MEETING

1. Pray for each Discipleship Group member by name, asking that each will want and develop a closer relationship with God.

2. In *Following Jesus*, complete Session 7, including the daily Bible study in 1 John and the prayer time.

3. Write specific prayer requests to share.

4. Gather materials for the meeting:
   • Bible
   • *Following Jesus*
   • *Time Alone With God Notebook* (your notes on 1 John)
   • Bible memory verses

THE MEETING

BUILDING THE GROUP (15 minutes)
Use the first five minutes to discuss any questions, problems, or observations the group members would like to share about their experiences with the daily time of Bible study and prayer.
Ask each person to name one characteristic of a close friendship. Suggest they write down each characteristic as it's mentioned. After everyone has contributed, discuss: **Which characteristics can immediately be**

identified as true of your relationship with God? Which cannot? Why? How does your relationship with your closest friend and your relationship with God differ?

 FOCUSING ON LIFE (10 minutes)
Discuss: **Do you think that prayer really changes things? Why? Name one experience you have had in your prayer life that resulted in change. How did that make you feel? Name one experience you have had when you felt that your prayer was not heard. How did you feel? Do you think God always answers your prayers? Someone once said, "Prayer doesn't change things; prayer changes people." Do you agree or disagree? Why?**

EXPLORING GOD'S WORD (20 minutes)
Allow several minutes for group members to review Session 7 and their written responses. Then discuss:
1. **When is the best time to pray?** (anytime, all the time)

2. **What kind of mood do you need to be in to pray effectively?** (It doesn't matter; moods do not affect the effectiveness of prayer [have students give examples from David's life]; God wants to hear from us when we're feeling good and when we're feeling discouraged or need help.)

3. **What are some things we can pray for?** *Refer to Matthew 6:9-14.* (daily needs, forgiveness, guidance, deliverance and protection, God's will to be done, God to be given glory)

4. **According to John 14:13, 15:7, and 16:24, what does God promise to do in response to our prayers?** (Give us whatever we ask.)

5. **What are the conditions attached to these promises?** (We must ask in His name and according to His will; we must obey His Word and pray with God's interests and kingdom in mind.)

6. **Why is prayer important for us as Christ's disciples?** (It's one of the only two ways we get to know and communicate with the Father - Master Teacher – God. Bible study is the other way.)
Discuss and say today's memory verse (John 16:24) together.

APPLYING GOD'S WORD (30 minutes)
It's important to learn about prayer, but it's more important to pray. Use the remaining time of this meeting for group prayer. Divide the prayer time into three parts:

1. Prayers of thanksgiving. Have each person share something with the group for which he is thankful today. Then ask everyone who will, to pray, thanking God for the things mentioned and anything else that comes to mind.

2. Prayers for personal needs. Ask that each person share personal prayer requests with the group. (You begin.) Again have a time of prayer when everyone who wants to can pray for the requests.

3. Prayers for others. Ask each person to suggest a prayer request for other people – your local church, local government, national issues, or world issues like hunger, peace, and justice. If they are familiar with any specific missionaries and mission work, include those too. Close the meeting by asking everyone to pray for one or more of the requests mentioned.

Assignments for Next Week: Be enthusiastic as you remind students to:

1. Complete Session 8.

2. Continue the daily Bible study and prayer time.

3. Review all Bible memory verses.

If any group members expressed significant problems when sharing prayer requests, try to talk with them before they leave the meeting or call them tomorrow. Assure them of your prayers and your availability to help them if you can.

AFTER THE MEETING

1. Evaluate: Were group members open and relaxed with one another during the prayer time? Was there evidence of their love and concern for one another as they discussed prayer requests and the things they were thankful for? If you're meeting for prayer before or after the last three meetings, plan ways to vary the prayer time. For example: (a) Have brief sentence prayers with each person adding to what the last person said. (b) Pray for one issue the entire time focusing on every aspect of it.

2. During the week, note specific answers to prayers offered today. Share them during the next prayer time.

S E S S I O N   8

In His Image

OVERVIEW

Key Concept   Spiritual growth is ongoing when we are committed to following Jesus regardless of the cost.

Memory Verse   Matthew 4:19

Goals   *Individual Growth:* To discover what it means to be a disciple and to decide to follow Christ daily as His obedient disciple.

                     Group Life: To learn the cost of following Christ as disciples and to begin to realize the benefits of having a group of loving, caring, forgiving friends who are on the same road.

BEFORE THE MEETING

1. Pray that each group member will have a strong and continual desire to follow Christ, whatever the cost.

2. In *Following Jesus*, complete Session 8, and continue the daily Bible study and prayer time.

3. If anyone in the group struggles with whether or not they are a sold out disciple, make it a priority to meet with him this week.

4. Gather the materials for the meeting:
   - Bible
   - *Following Jesus*
   - *Time Alone With God Notebook* (your notes on 1 John)
   - Bible memory verses

THE MEETING

 BUILDING THE GROUP (20 minutes)
Ask group members to share what they experienced as they continued their daily Bible study and prayer times. (For example: special insights from I John, answers to prayer, a fresh application during daily Bible study, triumphs or defeats in battling the daily time schedule, etc.) Discuss their reactions to the group prayer time last week. Would they like to have a similar time of prayer before or after each weekly meeting? If so, make plans to begin next week.

Give the group a few minutes to think about the different people who have influenced their Christian lives. These may be family members, personal friends or acquaintances, authors of books, radio or TV personalities, etc. Ask each one to share the name of one person and how or why that person has influenced him in his Christian walk. (Be prepared to share your own example first.)

 FOCUSING ON LIFE (10 minutes)
Say: **Almost everyone looks to someone or to some group for acceptance or direction. For example, think about some groups at your school. How can you tell which group a person belongs to? (Who he's with, how he acts, how he dresses, where he goes, etc.) Think about society as a whole. Where do most people get their ideas about what to do, what to wear, what to think and what to say? Who do people follow around and eagerly listen to? (TV and film stars, sports figures, politicians, musicians, disc jockeys, etc.) It's hard to find anyone who isn't patterning his life after someone or something. (Even people who claim to be "doing their own thing" are following a philosophy that's endorsed by many well-known people.) So the issue isn't so much whether we will follow anyone at all, but of whom will we choose to follow. Who is worthy to be followed?**

EXPLORING GOD'S WORD (30 minutes)
Allow a few minutes for group members to review Session 8 and their responses to it. Then discuss:

1. **According to your research this week, what is a disciple?** *Ask them to read their definitions. Then summarize:* **A disciple is one who learns, follows, and passes on what he has learned to others.**

2. What are the sure signs of being a disciple of Christ? *Refer to the list of characteristics from the Gospel of John, page 67.* (faith, knowledge of God's Word, obedience, love, unity with other disciples, fruit of the Spirit, caring for other people, etc.)

3. How do we become Christ's disciples? *Refer to Colossians 2:6; Hebrews 11:6.* (By faith, believing in Him.)

4. We all took that step when we became Christians. But, how do we continue on the road of discipleship without getting detoured? *See Colossians 2:7.* (We must be rooted in Christ, built up in Christ, strengthened in the faith, and overflowing with thanksgiving.)

5. Sounds good, doesn't it? But what do those words mean to us in real life? How do we become "rooted in Christ?" (through personal Bible study and prayer, and meditation — the underground "root system" of a strong Christian faith) **What can we do to be "built up in Christ"?** (Building up means to grow. We grow by applying God's Word to our lives, and by allowing Him to make us more like Christ.) **According to Colossians 3:12-16, what are some of these Christ-like qualities?** (compassion, kindness, humility, gentleness, patience, forgiveness, peaceableness, thankfulness, wisdom) **How are we strengthened in the faith?** (by meeting with other believers, hearing God's Word preached and discussed, reading books about the Christian life, etc.) **What will happen when we are "overflowing with thankfulness?"** (We will be telling other people about Christ and our lives in Him; we will be a source of encouragement and strength for other disciples; we will glorify God.)

6. What are some possible hindrances that could make it hard for you to stay on the road of discipleship? *Have the group refer to their responses on page 68.* How can they be overcome? (by Christ's power)

7. Christ has certainly promised that the life of discipleship will be worthwhile and full of benefits, but He never said it would be easy. According to Luke 9:23-26, what did He say is the cost of discipleship? *Refer to pages 69-70.*

8. Think about the examples we gave earlier of Christians who have encouraged us to keep on following Christ. In what ways do their lives show that they have paid the costs of obedient

discipleship? What can we learn from their examples of following Christ no matter what the costs?

 APPLYING GOD'S WORD (15 minutes)
Quote today's memory verse (Matthew 4:19) together. Then say: **Christ calls us all to follow Him as committed disciples. How will we respond?** Don't ask for verbal answers. Instead, allow a few minutes of silence so each group member can think through the implications of this study and pray about his commitment to be a 100-percent-sold-out disciple of Christ.

Refer to the "Making It Personal" section, page 72. Have each person review his response to the third assignment and write specific ways he thinks God wants to build these qualities into his life. Next, have several people share their responses to the fourth assignment – ways God can use them as disciples to share his life with others. Then as a group, discuss specific ways you can put these into practice this week.

Assignments for Next Week: Be enthusiastic as you give the following assignment.
1. Complete Session 9.

2. Continue daily Bible study and prayer time.

3. Review all Bible memory verses.

4. Talk with a non-Christian about your life in Christ.

AFTER THE MEETING

Evaluate: How did the group respond to this study? Is there a feeling of excitement? Are there any signs of fear? uncertainty? boredom? What are your feelings? How do you think your feelings affect the responses of the group members? Pray that God will give you a contagious enthusiasm for growing as a disciple and sharing your faith with others.

Blueprint for a Disciple

OVERVIEW

Key Concept   Spiritual growth is an adventure when we make decisions based on God's will.

Memory Verse   Proverbs 3:5-6

Goals   *Individual Growth:* To learn the principles that help us know God's will and to use them as we make decisions.

Group Life: To understand how important the counsel of other Christians becomes when we make decisions; to begin to ask for their prayers and counsel when we face hard decisions.

BEFORE THE MEETING

1. Pray for each member of the group by name, asking God to guide him in any decisions he is facing this week.

2. In *Following Jesus*, complete Session 9 and continue daily Bible study and prayer time.

3. Review all memory verses.

4. Tell someone you know who is not a Christian about your life in Christ. Be ready to share your experience with the group.

5. If the Discipleship Group agreed to meet for prayer before this week's meeting, call everyone to remind them to come 15 minutes early.

6. Gather materials for the meeting:
   - Bible
   - *Following Jesus*
   - *Time Alone With God Notebook* (your notes on 1 John)
   - Bible memory verses

THE MEETING

 BUILDING THE GROUP (15 minutes)
Ask various group members to recite one of the Bible memory verses. Do this until everyone recites at least two verses.

Ask volunteers to share their experiences this past week in talking to other people about their lives in Christ (include yourself). Ask: **What did you say? What was the person's response? How did you feel before and after? What has this experience taught you about the importance of talking about Christ to others?** There may be some in the group who didn't do this assignment because they were afraid; others may have had an unpleasant experience. Be understanding. Encourage them by saying that as they grow in Christ, sharing Him with others will become more natural and easy. Mention the rest of the books in the Moving Toward Maturity series. Emphasize how each book will help them grow in their relationships with God and in their ability and confidence to share Christ with others. (See the back cover of this Leader's Guide.)

FOCUSING ON LIFE (15 minutes)
Have each person share an important decision he has made in the past, telling how he made it and what happened as a result. Ask: **Are you confident that your decision was based on God's will? Not so sure? Sure it wasn't? Why do you feel the way you do?**

Ask: **Do you think God really cares about all of the details and decisions of our lives? Let's look at Psalm 139, Proverbs 5:21, and Matthew 6:25-34 to see.** *Briefly summarize the contents of each passage.* **What if we make a wrong turn?**

EXPLORING GOD'S WORD (25 minutes)
Have everyone review Session 9. Then discuss:
1. According to this week's study, what things do you know are God's will for every Christian? (He should be *saved* – looking to and believing in Christ; *sanctified* – living a holy and honorable life; *Spirit-filled; suffering* for doing good and enduring evil; *submitting* to God – obeying His written, known will.)

2. How can you find out what God wants you to do in a specific situation? *Refer to Proverbs 3:5-8.* (Trust God; consider all options and commit those options to God; leave the matter in God's hands; wait for God's answer; enjoy confidence in the decision.)

3. What do you usually think of when you talk to others about "God's will for my life"? (a life plan, career, etc.)

4. What do you think the Bible means when it speaks of "God's will" for your life? (a day-by-day decision to follow and obey God, not worrying about the future)

Have everyone read over the seven practical pointers for knowing God's will on page 82, under "Tips To Find God's Will." Briefly discuss each one.

APPLYING GOD'S WORD (20 minutes)
Ask volunteers to share difficult decisions they are facing right now. As each person describes the decision he needs to make, let other group members suggest options, mention Scriptures that apply, share their own experiences with similar decisions, and simply offer encouragement. After three or four people have received input on their particular decisions, ask each person to review what he wrote under the "Making It Personal" section, pages 80-81, regarding his own decision that needs to be made. Encourage each person to write down any new insights he has gained during this meeting that will help him in making that decision.

Recite today's memory verse (Proverbs 3:5-6) together. Then close the meeting in prayer. Ask several group members to pray specifically for the decisions that have been discussed.

Assignments for Next Week: Express your appreciation for the commitment of each person in the group, then remind them of what they need to do before the next meeting:
1. Complete Session 10.

2. Continue daily Bible study and prayer time. If you have finished the 1 John study, you may want to begin studying the Gospel of John at your own rate.

3. Review all Bible memory verses.

AFTER THE MEETING

Evaluate: Did everyone get involved in today's discussions? Was there an atmosphere of warmth, caring, and true concern when group members shared decisions they were facing? Did you let group members counsel one another without stepping in too quickly with your own suggestions?

Good, Better, Best

OVERVIEW

Key Concept   Spiritual growth is increased when we set our priorities on God's purposes for our lives.

Memory Verse   Matthew 6:33

Goals   *Individual Growth:* To set specific goals for spiritual growth, plan the steps needed to meet those goals, and begin taking those steps.

Group Life: To set goals for the group and plan how to reach them as well as to encourage each other in individual goals.

BEFORE THE MEETING

1. Pray for each person in the group, asking that God will guide him in his study as he plans goals and sets priorities for his life. Pray that the group as a whole will continue as a growing, maturing body of believers.

2. In *Following Jesus*, complete Session 10 and continue the daily Bible study and prayer time.

3. Call each group member during the week and ask him to be thinking of goals he would like the group itself to set and move toward. Ask him to pray about renewing his commitment to continue in the Discipleship Group.

4. List the goals you would like the group to reach in the coming weeks.

5. Gather materials for the meeting:
   - Bible
   - *Following Jesus*
   - *Time Alone With God Notebook* (your notes on 1 John)
   - Bible memory verses
   - *Spending Time Alone with God* – the next book in the Moving Toward Maturity Series

THE MEETING

BUILDING THE GROUP (20 minutes)

Since this is the last meeting in this introductory discipleship study, ask all the people in the group to share specific things they have appreciated about being part of a Discipleship Group. Then ask what they liked best and least about the book, *Following Jesus*; about the group meetings; about the assignments; etc.

After everyone has shared their thoughts, have a brief time of prayer, thanking God for allowing each one the opportunity to be a part of this group and for teaching you important truths.

Review the main points of the past nine Bible studies by asking:
1. **How can we know we are truly Christians?**
2. **What are three purposes God has for our lives?**
3. **What are five characteristics of God's love?**
4. **Why is it important for Christians to love other people?**
5. **What are the results of Christ living in us and we in Him?**
6. **What five things can we do to get to know God's Word?**
7. **Why is prayer an important part of a Christian's life?**
8. **What are sure signs of being a disciple?**
9. **How can we find God's will in specific situations?**

Recite the first nine memory verses together.

FOCUSING ON LIFE (10 minutes)

Say: **Are you ever overwhelmed with all the things you have to do each week? Do you ever wish you had 30-hour days or 8-day weeks? Everyone has the same number of hours each day, so the difference between a person who accomplishes a great deal in his life and one who barely manages to survive must be in the ways each chooses to spend his time. Let's see where our time is going, by checking out how we spent the 168 hours of each week.**

Have everyone write the number of hours they spent sleeping, in school, eating meals, studying, etc. Then have them total their hours. Most of them will have 20 or so hours unaccounted for. Suggest that it is how they spend those unaccounted hours that will determine whether they reach the goals they set for themselves in this week's session.

EXPLORING GOD'S WORD (25 minutes)
Give everyone a few minutes to review Session 10 and their written responses. Then discuss:

1. What are some of the world's definitions of "success"?
(attainment of wealth, fame, or power)

2. What is your definition of "success"? *Refer them to their written response on page 83.*

3. How will we know when we become successful? (by reaching set goals; following priorities)

4. As disciples, what should be our first concern when we begin to set goals for our lives? (finding out what God's goals are for us)

5. What are some of God's goals for us as His disciples? (seeking His kingdom, being conformed to His image, doing everything for His glory, knowing Christ, becoming like Christ)

Ask two or three people to share the life goal each wrote for himself on page 84. (You go first.) Discuss: **What does this goal mean in day-to-day living? How will it affect the way you live? What habits will you have to change to make it happen?**

Discuss how the commitment and goals accomplished by the Discipleship Group during the past ten weeks have changed their lives: **What are some things that happened as a result of spending a specific amount of time each day in Bible study and prayer? What encouraged you to finish the Bible study assignment before each meeting? How did you resolve the conflict when another activity was scheduled at the same time the Discipleship Group met?**

Impress on the group that this week's study is about *life* goals, *life* commitment, *life* changes – not short-term activities. Discuss how, as a result of keeping their commitments to the group and achieving the goals that were set, they now have a positive foundation on which to build life goals.

APPLYING GOD'S WORD (20 minutes)
Share your list of priorities from before and after you put Christ first in your life. Explain why you made the changes you did. Ask who else would like to share his priority list, or if anyone has a question about how to set priorities. Say: **All parts of our lives – mental, spiritual, social, and physical – are important to Christ. Playing basketball, learning to play the piano, studying French, going to parties,**

taking walks, etc. – everything we do can be done for the glory of God. He made us the way we are so that we can do all those things and have fellowship with Him. Quote today's memory verse (Matthew 6:33) together.

Since this is the last week in this particular study, ask people in the group to suggest future goals for the group itself. Do they want to continue as a "group"? Describe the next book in the Moving Toward Maturity series, *Spending Time Alone with God.* Suggest that studying it together would be a good way to build on the foundation established during the past few weeks of work and study. How can the group, as a part of the body of Christ, fulfill the goals that God has for it (seeking His kingdom, knowing Christ, and making Him known)?

Ask them if they want to review their commitments to this Discipleship Group or to stop meeting. If they decide to continue, challenge each one to be faithful to God and to the group. Determine how soon, when, and where they would like to begin the study of *Spending Time Alone With God.* (They may need a brief break.) Make sure they have completed all assignments in *Following Jesus* before beginning the studies in *Spending Time Alone with God.*

Close the meeting with a time of prayer. Ask for specific requests any of them may have; then have several volunteers pray.

Try to talk with everyone individually before leaving the meeting. Thank each one for his faithfulness to the group and encourage each one to continue to be a part of whatever the Discipleship Group decides to do. Also encourage each to continue with a personal time of Bible study and prayer.

No Assignment

AFTER THE MEETING

If the group set a time to begin a study of *Spending Time Alone with God,* be sure to call everyone during the week to remind them of where and when to meet.

SPENDING TIME ALONE WITH GOD

Leader's Guide prepared by
Barry St. Clair and Juanita Wright Potter

Leading Your Discipleship Group

Moving Toward Maturity is a five-part discipleship training series for young people. It is designed to help them become independently dependent on Jesus Christ and then teach others to do the same. This series has four main purposes:

      1. To encourage students to passionately pursue Jesus Christ.
      2. To help young people develop strong, Christ-like character.
      3. To train young people in the "how to's" of Christian living.
      4. To move young people from the point of getting to know Jesus Christ to the point of offering Him to others.

Spending Time Alone with God, the second book in the series, will challenge students to develop intimacy with God through daily time alone with God. Through Bible study and prayer, students will discover how to draw near to God – basic in growing as a disciple of Jesus Christ.

The other four study books in the series and related materials are described on the outside back cover of this Leader's Guide.

IMPORTANT NOTE: This Leader's Guide contains vital instructions, hints, and direction to help you lead your group most effectively. **We have placed this important information in only one place in the Leader's Guide, pages 7-11 in the *Following Jesus* section of the Leader's Guide.** Each time you begin a new book, review thoroughly the "Leading Your Discipleship Group" material. By doing so, you will sharpen your own leadership abilities. Through God's Spirit and your investment, students' lives will change.

SCRIPTURE MEMORY NOTE: Each Moving Toward Maturity book contains Bible memory verses that students memorize each week. These verses are found on the last page of each book. Since students tend to have trouble memorizing verses, your encouragement will help them succeed. The design of these books does not allow us to provide removable Scripture memory cards. Help by giving them ten small blank cards with a rubber band. Each week, when you make the assignments, have them write out the verse for the week on the card. Encourage them to carry the verses with them to review during the week. Keep extra cards in case they lose them. Helping your students succeed in memorizing Scripture is one of the greatest gifts you can give them!

INTRODUCTORY SESSION

Continuing Your Discipleship Group

OVERVIEW

Key Concept   To benefit most from a group study of *Spending Time Alone with God,* we must wholeheartedly enter into the disciplines of a Discipleship Group.

Goals   *Individual Growth:* To accept the privileges and responsibilities of the Discipleship Group for another 10-week period.

Group Life: To continue to build the strong relationships within the group established during the *Following Jesus* group experience.

BEFORE THE MEETING

1. Study pages 7-11 of this Leader's Guide for important background information.

2. In *Spending Time Alone with God,* study pages 1-11, and put together the memory verse packet located in the back of the book.

3. Call each person who said he would come to the first meeting. This will consist of students who went through *Following Jesus.* Ask everyone to bring their school and work schedules.

4. Be prepared to present the purpose and format of the Moving Toward Maturity series to the group. Place special emphasis on the content of *Spending Time Alone with God.*

5. Gather materials for the meeting:
   - Bible
   - *Spending Time Alone with God*
   - 3"x 5" cards
   - Pencils

• Bible memory verses
• *Time Alone with God Notebook*

THE MEETING

BUILDING THE GROUP (20 minutes)
As each person arrives, greet him warmly. Ask each person to update addresses, phone, and e-mail.

When everyone has arrived, ask each person to think of three words that describe himself. Ask each person to share his three words with the rest of the group.

FOCUSING ON LIFE (5 minutes)
Discuss: **What factors in our lives help determine the kinds of persons we become?** (parents, teachers, natural abilities, etc.) **What tools does God use to mold each of us into the person He wants us to be?** (Scripture, tests of faith, trials, fellowship with other Christians, etc.) Write down their responses to this question to use later in "Considering the Choice."

EXPLORING THE CHALLENGE (20 minutes)
Have a volunteer read 1 Corinthians 12:12-20, 27. Share with the group that God has designed the body of Christ in such a way that Christians need each other. Through fellowship, the members of the body give each other insight, support, and encouragement. Emphasize that being part of a Discipleship Group is an excellent way to connect ourselves to the body of Christ.

Review the purpose of the Moving Toward Maturity series (page 52 of the Leader's Guide). Let each student express something he learned or experienced from being in a previous Discipleship Group.

Give everyone a copy of *Spending Time Alone with God*. Collect the money for this book and the *Time Alone with God Notebook* when you give them out. Review the topics to be discussed, and read the group disciplines (pages 11-12). Also hand out the *Time Alone with God Notebooks*. Explain that they will not be used until next week's session. Provide an opportunity for any questions concerning the commitment to or the responsibilities of becoming a part of the Discipleship Group. (NOTE: Even though the group may want to continue as a Discipleship Group after studying *Spending Time Alone with God,* they are only being asked to consider a commitment for the next ten weeks.)

Briefly review the length and number of meetings (one to one and a half hours per week with the group, plus individual study time, for the next ten weeks). Then have everyone consult their schedules and decide on a specific time and place to meet. Also schedule dates for your fun activity and half day of prayer (see page 89), but don't discuss specific plans at this time.

CONSIDERING THE CHOICE (15 minutes)
Review the list you compiled earlier of things God uses to influence our lives. Ask the group which of these ways God could use to give their lives direction through this Discipleship Group.

Challenge the group to think and pray about making another 10-week commitment to the Discipleship Group. Be sure they understand that this time they will be expected to have a daily time alone with God. Anyone who decides not to become a part of this particular Discipleship Group should let you know before the next meeting and return his unmarked set of materials. Those who choose to join should complete Session 1 in *Spending Time Alone with God* before the next meeting.

Encourage everyone to set aside a specific time each week to complete the Bible study for the next Discipleship Group meeting.

Close with a prayer. Pray for each person to make a wise decision about joining the Discipleship Group. Thank God for what He is going to do in all of your lives as you commit yourselves to Him and to each other.

Assignments for Next Week: Give the following assignments to those who decide to join the Discipleship Group:
1. In *Spending Time Alone with God*, read pages 9-12, study and sign the "Personal Commitment" sheet (page 13).

2. Complete Session 1 (down to the *Assignment* section), and put together the memory verse packet in the back of the book. (Show the group your packet to demonstrate what it looks like put together.)

Memorize Mark 1:35, as indicated in the *Making it Personal*

section of Session 1.

3. Bring a Bible, a pen or pencil, *Spending Time Alone with God,* **and your** *Time Alone with God Notebook* **to every meeting.**

Also remind the group to bring enough money next week to reimburse you for the student book and notebook, if they have not done so.

As students leave, try to talk with them individually. See if they have any questions or problems. Let them know you care about each of them and their concerns.

AFTER THE MEETING

1. Evaluate: Did each person become involved in sharing his ideas and feelings? How can you more effectively involve each person in next week's discussion? Review "Effective Meetings," pages 10-11 of this Leader's Guide.

2. This week, and every week, begin preparing for the next session at least five days in advance. Complete Session 1 in *Spending Time Alone with God,* and read through the Leader's Guide suggestions.

Getting to Know Him

OVERVIEW

Key Concept   A daily time alone with God causes us to draw near to God.

Memory Verse   Mark 1:35

Goals   *Individual Growth:* To learn how to develop intimacy with God by spending time alone with God each day.

Group Life: To agree to support and encourage one another as a Discipleship Group for the next ten weeks.

BEFORE THE MEETING

1. Pray for each person who came to the last meeting, asking God to give each one a deep desire to know Him.

2. In *Spending Time Alone with God*, do Session 1, writing down your personal responses to each question. Each week, note in the margins other observations or personal experiences that relate to the lesson and bring them up during the group meeting.

3. Memorize Mark 1:35.

4. Telephone each group member, reminding him of the place and time for the meeting. Answer any questions students have. If someone has decided not to participate in the Discipleship Group, assure him that you still care for him, and express hope that he will be able to participate in a future group.

5. Complete the list of the names, addresses, phone numbers, and e-mail addresses of all the group members. Make copies for each person.

6. Examine your own relationship with God. Pray for motivation and diligence to strengthen your personal time alone with God.

7. Gather materials for the meeting:
- Bible
- *Spending Time Alone with God*
- List of group members' names addresses, phone numbers, and e-mails
- Bible memory verses
- *Time Alone with God Notebook*
- One sheet of 5-1/2" x 8-1/2"paper for each group member

THE MEETING

BUILDING THE GROUP (15 minutes)
Greet each person. Welcome him as an important member of the group.

Confirm that by each person's presence, he is saying, "Yes, I want to be a part of this Discipleship Group." Have everyone turn to the *Personal Commitment* sheet (page 13, *Spending Time Alone with God*). Read it aloud. Then ask anyone who hasn't already done so to sign his sheet. (Be sure to sign yours too!) Pass the books around and ask each person to sign the others' books.

Have someone read Hebrews 10:24-25. Ask volunteers to share how they think these verses can apply to the Discipleship Group. Challenge the group to begin to encourage one another – in their time alone with God, in their witness at school, and in their relationships with others. Offer short prayers asking God: (1) To deepen each person's intimacy in his relationship to Christ and his commitment to the Discipleship Group, and (2) to develop a closeness between the group members.

FOCUSING ON LIFE (15 minutes)
Discuss: **Has there ever been someone you've really wanted to get to know? Why? How did you go about trying to get to know that person? What questions did you ask? What did you tell him about yourself?**

What has God done to encourage us to get to know Him? (gave us the Bible; sent Jesus; provided Christian friends, etc.) **How can we respond to God's desire to get to know us?** (receiving Jesus Christ; spending time with the Lord in prayer; reading the Bible, etc.)

Emphasize that spending time alone with God is not a duty or a demand, but rather an opportunity to get to know the Lord of the universe in a more intimate way.

EXPLORING GOD'S WORD (20 minutes)

(NOTE: *Each week this section is based on the work students have done in* Spending Time Alone with God. *The discussion questions are usually not identical to those in the study book, but they draw from the same Scriptures and assignments. This technique helps students think through what they've studied rather than just parroting written answers.*)

Allow time for group members to review their answers and comments for Session 1 in *Spending Time Alone with God.* Encourage them to ask questions and make observations. Then discuss these questions:

1. According to Hebrews 4:12, in what ways can God's Word penetrate our lives? Then what benefits result from spending time in God's Word? (the Word of God comes alive; God digs down deep in our lives; our motivations become more clear; we see our thoughts and interests compared to God's thoughts and interests, etc.)

2. According to John 4:23 what kind of people does God want to worship Him? How does he desire those people to worship Him? (in spirit and truth) **How does this verse apply to spending time alone with God?** (Our desire to spend time with God comes from our hearts and leads us to the truth.)

3. Have someone read Hosea 6:6. **What makes God happy?** (our knowledge of Him) **How can your time alone with God deepen your knowledge of Him?**

To affirm each person's desire for a daily time alone with God, quote the memory verse (Mark 1:35) together.

APPLYING GOD'S WORD (20 minutes)

Have the group recall any problems they have experienced in trying to draw close to God - struggles praying, being obedient to God, or studying the Bible. Ask volunteers to share their struggles. (Start with Sam's experience described on page 18 of *Spending Time Alone with God,* or give an example from your own life.) Then discuss how spending time alone with God each day can overcome these struggles.

Ask each person to write: (1) one way he will develop the discipline of spending time alone with God this week (Examples: Go to bed earlier;

set two alarms; find a private place with no interruptions.) (2) one way he will encourage another person to have his time alone with God (Examples: Check with him each day about his time alone with God; call at a set time in the morning to make sure he is up).

Ask each person to pray for the person on his right; that he would begin to have a meaningful and regular time alone with God, resulting in deeper intimacy in his walk with the Lord. (If students are shy about praying aloud, talk to them individually and challenge them to prepare this week to take part in future group prayer time.)

Assignments for Next Week: Positively present the following assignments. Let the students know that you can see their desire to deepen their relationship to Christ.
1. Complete Session 1 in *Spending Time Alone with God.*

2. Learn the memory verse and use the daily Scripture readings for your time alone with God.

3. Begin using your *Time Alone with God Notebook.* **Use what you learned this week during this Discipleship Group meeting. Put those ideas into practice this week, and be prepared to tell how they worked.**

AFTER THE MEETING

1. Evaluate: Was the atmosphere relaxed? Did everyone take part? If not, jot down some ways you can improve the next group meeting. If any students were silent, you may want to spend time with them this week to get to know them better.

2. Familiarize yourself with the planned half day of prayer at the end of the 10-week study (see page 89). Begin to pray now for this special day during your daily time alone with God.

3. Think about the group outing (picnic, hike, swimming, etc.) that will build relationships with the group.

4. If possible, meet with some members of the group this week – separately, or two or three together – to build relationships.

S E S S I O N   2

Build the Relationship

OVERVIEW

Key Concept   Consistently spending time alone with God results in a deepening relationship with God.

Memory Verse   2 Timothy 3:16

Goals   *Individual Growth:* To discover and put into practice a specific plan for spending time alone with God daily.

Group Life: To encourage one another to faithfully spend time alone with God.

BEFORE THE MEETING

1. Pray for each group member by name, asking God to make you aware of his particular needs.

2. In *Spending Time Alone with God,* complete Bible study 2 and the daily assignments from Bible study 1.

3. Memorize 2 Timothy 3:16.

4. E-mail each group member, reminding him of your prayers, and encouraging him to continue his daily time alone with God.

5. Gather materials for the meeting:
   • Bible
   • *Spending Time Alone with God*
   • Bible memory verses
   • *Time Alone with God Notebook*

THE MEETING

BUILDING THE GROUP (15 minutes)
Ask volunteers to tell what they did this past week to (1) get motivated to have a time alone with God, and (2) encourage another group member to do the same.

Then discuss: **Have you ever been in love or thought you were? Did you let the other person know? How did you feel when you caught a glimpse of that person coming toward you, and knew you were going to get a chance to talk? Do you think you could ever have the same kind of eager expectation and excitement about getting to talk to God? Why or why not?**

FOCUSING ON LIFE (25 minutes)

Allow time for group members to review their answers and comments for Session 2 in *Spending Time Alone with God.* Encourage them to ask questions and make observations. Then discuss these questions:

1. **In Jeremiah 29:12-14, God says that He will listen to us and will let us find Him. However, He requires some things from us before that can happen. What are they?** (call upon Him; pray to Him; seek Him with all our heart)

2. **What do you think it means to seek God with all your heart?** (to desire to know Him better than anyone else; to make Him the most important priority in your life) **How does that relate to having a time alone with God?**

3. **What does 2 Timothy 3:16 say about the Bible?** (All Scripture is God-breathed; it is useful for teaching; it rebukes; it corrects; it trains in righteousness.) **What are the benefits of allowing God to correct, rebuke, teach, and train us through Scripture?** (See 2 Timothy 3:17. We become equipped for every good work.)

Quote 2 Timothy 3:16 together as a group.

APPLYING GOD'S WORD (10 minutes)

Have the group discuss their first week of spending time alone with God. **Was it an awkward experience or a smooth one (or both)? Was it hard to meet with God every day? Did anyone miss a day or two? What problems did you encounter?**

Make a list of these problems, and then brainstorm ways to overcome them. Ask the group to help each other in solving these problems.

Divide into pairs and have partners pray for each other, asking God to help each one overcome specific obstacles that stand in the way of a successful time alone with God.

(NOTE: *Not every session in this Leader's Guide will include a group discussion of individual times alone with God. However, it will keep your students on track if you take a few minutes each week to ask about their daily times with God. You want to see if anyone is having difficulty or needs help.*)

1. Complete Session 2 in *Spending Time Alone with God*.

2. Spend time alone with God every school day this week.
(Review this assignment with the group. Make sure everyone understands how to fill out their Bible Response sheets. Then remind them to complete one every day during the next week.)

3. Learn the memory verse - Joshua 1:8.

4. Be ready to talk about positive steps you've taken to overcome your personal struggles in spending time alone with God.

AFTER THE MEETING

1. Evaluate: Is the group continuing to develop closeness? Was the group relaxed and comfortable? Did everyone participate? If not, perhaps something as simple as having soft drinks or hot chocolate before the meeting would help.

2. Are students coming to the meetings with their assignments completed? Give encouragement as needed, with a phone call, e-mail, or personal appointment.

3. If anyone seems overwhelmed with daily spending time alone with God, meet with him sometime this week and do it together.

4. Continue to plan a group outing for sometime during the next two weeks and the half day of prayer after Session 10.

Learn the Word

OVERVIEW

Key Concept   Studying God's Word helps us get to know ourselves and Jesus better.

Memory Verse   Joshua 1:8

Goals   *Individual Growth:* To understand how to study God's Word.

Group Life: To encourage one another to get into the Bible every day.

BEFORE THE MEETING

1. Ask God to give each group member a deep trust in and love for His Word.

2. *In Spending Time Alone with God,* complete Session 3.

3. Memorize Joshua 1:8.

4. Gather materials for the meeting:
   - Bible
   - *Spending Time Alone with God*
   - Bible memory verses
   - *Time Alone with God Notebook*
   - Extra paper

THE MEETING

BUILDING THE GROUP (20 minutes)
Ask the group to imagine this situation: **You have fallen in love with someone. You know a lot about him (her), but this person barely knows you. And you've decided to write him (her) a love letter.**

Pass out extra paper to anyone who needs it. Allow three to five minutes for each group member to write a fictitious love letter. Then ask two or three volunteers to read their letters. As a group, discuss the contents of the letters. **What did these letter writers tell about themselves? In what ways is God's Word a love letter to us? What similarities does the Bible have to the love letters that were read to the group? What differences?**

FOCUSING ON LIFE (15 minutes)

Discuss: **Have you ever been confused about the question, "Who am I?" Not in the sense of "I'm a boy, son of Mr. Smith, 5'8", good looking"; but rather, "Who am I, deep down inside?"** Allow two or three volunteers to respond.

Then ask: **Have you ever been confused about what God is like, perhaps as a result of some seemingly senseless tragedy (a death, personal failure, etc.)?** Give an example from your own life or again ask for volunteers. Let the group grapple with the questions for a while before continuing. Then have them look up Hebrews 4:12 and James 1:23-24. Ask: **What can we discover about ourselves from God's Word?** (our true attitudes and our thoughts) Point out that the Bible works as a mirror to show us who we really are.

What does the Bible reveal about God? (His character over the ages; His love for the world and the sending of His Son; His perfect qualities; how He has been involved with mankind throughout history)

EXPLORING GOD'S WORD (30 minutes)

Allow time for the group to review their answers and comments from Session 3 in *Spending Time Alone with God*. Encourage them to ask questions and make observations. Then discuss these questions:

1. **What are some results of spending time in God's Word?** (getting to know yourself better; knowing Jesus better; growth as a believer; a fruitful life; ability to handle temptation)

2. **Define a "fruitful life."** (Refer to Psalm 1:1-3.)

3. **Psalms 1:3 refers to a "tree planted by streams of water." Jeremiah 17:8 further describes characteristics of a tree planted by water. How do these passages apply to a Christian's life?** (overcoming temptation and stress; turning worry to faith when circumstances look bad; "fruit" is produced)

4. What are some reasons, found in Session 3, that let us know why we can trust the Bible? (The human authors were eyewitnesses of the events they wrote about – 2 Peter 1:16 and 1 John 1:1-3; the writers investigated the facts before writing – Luke 1:1-4; the Bible is inspired by God – 2 Timothy 3:16; the whole Bible, though written by many different human authors who lived hundreds of years apart, fits together as a single expression of God's truth – Psalm 119:160.)

Quote Joshua 1:8 together, making note of the commands as well as the promises that are included in the verse.

APPLYING GOD'S WORD (10 minutes)
Have a volunteer quote 2 Timothy 3:16 (last session's memory verse). Then have each person make two columns in Spending *Time Alone with God* or on a piece of paper with the headings, "Training in Righteousness" and "Areas Needing Correction." Any personal characteristics he needs to acquire or develop should go in the first column. Any bad habits or attitudes that need correction should be listed in the second.

After completing the list, have each student select the one characteristic he most wants to acquire and the one attitude or habit he most wants to improve. Close with prayer asking God to change those areas of each person's life. Each student pray for the person on his or her right.

Assignments for Next Week:
1. Complete Session 4

2. Learn the memory verse - Psalms 119:9-11.

3. Spend time alone with God every school day this week.

AFTER THE MEETING

1. Evaluate: Is any student dominating the group time? If so, tactfully suggest that he give the less vocal members an opportunity to share.

2. If anyone is still coming unprepared or is slack in his assignments, get together with him this week to see if you can get to the reason he is struggling. Ask God to help you determine if it is a deeper issue or just a lack of discipline. Address the issue accordingly.

3. Your special outing should take place this week or next. Plan it well. Use the time to strengthen relationships.

4. Continue to pray for and plan the half day of prayer.

S E S S I O N   4

Hide the Word

OVERVIEW

Key Concept   Scripture memory equips us with God's way of thinking.

Memory Verse   Psalm 119:9-11

Goals   *Individual Growth:* To discover the value and discipline of
                     Scripture memory.

                     Group Life: To develop a positive attitude toward
                     Scripture memory.

BEFORE THE MEETING

1. Pray that God will give each person enjoyment and persistence in
   memorizing Scripture.

2. In *Spending Time Alone with God*, complete Session 4.

3. Memorize Psalm 119:9-11.

4. Gather materials for the meeting:
   - Bible
   - *Spending Time Alone with God*
   - Bible memory verses
   - *Time Alone with God Notebook*
   - Two road maps—one intact, and one with several holes
        cut in it
   - Bible concordance

THE MEETING

BUILDING THE GROUP (20 minutes)
Divide into two groups. Give one group an intact road map. Give the
second group an identical map, except with a few large holes in it.
Ask both groups to chart the best route from one major city to another.

After three minutes, ask one person from each group to describe the route his group took. (The second group should describe a much more complicated route because of the detours forced by the holes.) Discuss: **In what way(s) is the Bible a road map for our lives? What happens when we try to plan our lives with an incomplete knowledge of God's Word?** (Our lives become unnecessarily complicated.)

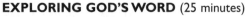

FOCUSING ON LIFE (15 minutes)
Discuss the following questions:
Have you ever been faced with a tough decision and you didn't have any idea what to do? (Share a personal example or ask volunteers to do so.)

How did you finally make the decision? (pressure from friends; advice from parents; flipped a coin; took no action, etc.)

What difference would it have made if you had known what God had to say about that situation?

EXPLORING GOD'S WORD (25 minutes)
Allow time for the group to review their answers and comments from Session 4 in *Spending Time Alone with God*. Let them ask questions and make observations. Then discuss these questions:
1. What positive ways does memorizing Scripture help you? (makes the Bible come alive; keeps you spiritually strong in everyday situations; helps you prosper spiritually; helps you overcome temptation; helps you be a more effective witness for Christ; changes the way you think)

2. Which of those benefits means the most to you personally and why?

3. What are three reasons you *can* memorize Scripture? (your memory is good; a right attitude makes a difference; you have what you need)

4. Ask volunteers to share how they completed the sentence, "I can memorize Scripture because..." on page 44 of this week's Bible study.

Have the group recite Psalm 119:9-11, and emphasize the reasons given in those verses for developing the discipline of Scripture memory.

 **APPLYING GOD'S WORD** (15 minutes)
As a group, make a list of problems that young people frequently
face. Select one that is common to most of your students. Use a
Bible concordance to find Scripture passages that apply directly to the
problem, having group members read each passage aloud. (Make sure
everyone knows how to use a concordance.)

Encourage students to use this method whenever they face problems in
the future. Challenge them to memorize at least one verse that relates to
that problem. Then whenever the same problem arises again, they will
have God's Word with them to give them guidance.

Assignments for Next Week
1. Complete Session 5 in *Spending Time Alone with God*.

2. Be prepared to recite the memory verse, John 15:7.

3. Spend time alone with God at least six days this week.

AFTER THE MEETING

1. Evaluate: Are your students enthusiastic about Scripture memory? If
anyone seems indifferent, set up a time to talk with him and find out why.

2. Are you giving group members plenty of time to express themselves,
and not dominating the meeting yourself?

3. Arrange to spend some time with two or three group members this
week, to get to know them better.

4. Prepare to announce the half day of prayer at the next meeting.

Talk With God

OVERVIEW

Key Concept   Talking to God in prayer is a privilege that allows us to draw near to Him.

Memory Verse   John 15:7

Goals   *Individual Goals:* To begin drawing near to God by spending time with Him in prayer.

Group Life: To recognize the value of prayer as a means for encouraging each other.

BEFORE THE MEETING

1. Spend some time in prayer, asking God to make your own time alone with Him such a vital part of your life that the group can tell how important it is to you.

2. In *Spending Time Alone with God,* complete Session 5.

3. Memorize John 15:7.

4. Gather materials for the meeting:
   - Bible
   - *Spending Time Alone with God*
   - Memorize John 15:7
   - *Time Alone with God Notebook*

THE MEETING

 BUILDING THE GROUP (25 minutes)
Ask each person to recite John 15:7. Have each one express ways God used this verse to apply to specific situations he has faced this week.

Since this is the halfway point of your Discipleship Group meetings, ask the group to evaluate the meetings so far: what they have liked best, what they have liked least, etc.

Review the main points of the past four weeks with the following:

(1) What is the purpose of having a time alone with God? (See Session 1.)

(2) What are some actions or attitudes we need in order to build a relationship with God? (See Session 2.)

(3) What are the results of spending time in God's Word? (See Session 3.)

(4) What are the benefits of memorizing Scripture? (See Session 4.)

Recite together the memory verses from the first four Sessions.

Ask the group to pray sentence prayers, renewing their desire to draw near to God and their commitment to encourage each other for the next five weeks. Close the prayer, asking God to continue to lead each student into a more intimate relationship with Jesus.

 FOCUSING ON LIFE (15 minutes)
Discuss: **Have you ever had someone make and then break a promise to you? How did you feel? What was your response? How did you react to that person's promises later on?**

When God makes a promise, what can we expect to happen? (Have volunteers give personal examples of how God has kept His promises to them.)

Does experiencing God's faithfulness in the past make you trust Him more?

Explain to the group that God is the only One who is completely trustworthy. He will never fail us. He may not give the answer we expect, or do exactly what we want, but He will never break His promises or forsake us.

 EXPLORING GOD'S WORD (25 minutes)
Allow time for the group to review their answers and comments from Session 5 in *Spending Time Alone with God*. Encourage them to ask questions and make observations. Then discuss these questions:

1. What are the purposes of prayer?

2. Have someone read 2 Peter 3:18. What was Peter's prayer for these people? How do you think we go about "growing in the grace and knowledge of our Lord and Savior?" (primarily through prayer and Bible study)

3. What answers can God give us when we pray? (Yes. No. Wait.) **Why does He answer in each of those ways?**

4. Jesus says that the heart of prayer is to "remain in Me and My words remain in you" (John 15:7). **What does it mean to remain (or abide) in Christ?** (Refer to John 15:4, 5, 10.) **How can spending time with God in prayer help us remain in Him?**

Recite John 15:7 together and note the result of remaining in Christ.

APPLYING GOD'S WORD (15 minutes)
Have each person list in his *Time Alone with God Notebook* the "Top Three" concerns in his life. Ask the students to express the prayer requests they have listed. Ask them to pray over those concerns every day in light of John 15:7. Ask them to take notes on what God does with each of those concerns this week.

Assignments for Next Week:
1. Complete Session 6.

2. Memorize Psalms 146:1-2.

3. Focus on prayer during your time alone with God this week. Pray for your "Top Three" concerns in light of John 15:7.

ANNOUNCE
At this time, announce the half day of prayer at the end of the study of *Spending Time Alone with God.* Briefly describe the events to take place, and make sure the date you have set is still a good one for each person.

AFTER THE MEETING

Evaluate: How did your group members seem to respond to this session on prayer?

Do they seem to have a desire to talk to God, or do they see prayer as a chore? Are they comfortable when asked to pray aloud? If not, encourage them to participate in simple, brief sentence prayers. Try to provide opportunities for them to pray in a group with as little pressure as possible. Teach them by example. If your prayers are usually long and eloquent, students may be intimidated when they are asked to pray. Keep it short!

S E S S I O N 6

Praise the Lord!

OVERVIEW

Key Concept   Praise focuses us on who God is and our time alone
with God gives us an opportunity to praise Him.

Memory Verse   Psalm 146:1-2

Goals   *Individual Growth:* To discover the importance of praising
God every day, and to develop an attitude of praise that
penetrates our lives.

Group Life: To practice praise in our Discipleship Group,
so it becomes a natural part of our lives.

BEFORE THE MEETING

1. Pray for the individual needs of group members. Ask God to give each
person a desire to praise God from an understanding of His character.

2. In *Spending Time Alone with God,* complete Session 6.

3. Memorize Psalm 146:1-2.

4. Focus on praise during your personal prayer and Bible study times this
week.

5. Gather materials for the meeting:
   • Bible
   • *Spending Time Alone with God*
   • Bible memory verses
   • *Time Alone with God Notebook*
   • Refreshments

THE MEETING

BUILDING THE GROUP (20 minutes)

Greet each person as he arrives. Serve refreshments and spend about five minutes hanging out. Then begin the meeting by asking each person to pick one of his "top three" concerns and tell how John 15:7 applied to that concern this last week.

Then ask each person to point out one positive characteristic of the person on his left. After everyone has had a turn, ask: **How did you feel when you were praised for your good qualities? What are some of the characteristics of God that are worthy of praise?** (After people respond, ask someone to read Revelation 4:11.)

FOCUSING ON LIFE (10 minutes)

Discuss the following questions:

1. When did you feel your best this past week? At that point, how did you respond to God and to others around you?

2. When did you feel your worst this past week? What made you feel that way? At that point, how did you respond to God and to others? Is it harder to praise God when things aren't going well?

Explain that even though God may not have directly caused the unpleasant situations, He can use them for our good. The secret of being able to praise God at all times is realizing who He is. He is always faithful and His character never changes. He will never fail us.

EXPLORING GOD'S WORD (35 minutes)

Allow time for the group to review their answers and comments for Session 7 in *Spending Time Alone with God.* Encourage them to ask questions and make observations. Then discuss these questions:

1. How does praise affect how we handle problems? (Refer to the "gaze/glance" sections of this week's study.)

2. What are some elements of praise found in Psalm 105:1-4? (Refer to subhead on pages 59-61, "Learning How to Express Praise.") **Which of these elements is the most meaningful to you? Why?**

3. One thing that can help us praise God when we're in difficult situations is remembering how He has worked in our lives in the

past. What are some ways God has "shown up" during difficult times?

Recite Psalm 146:1-2 together as a commitment to live with an attitude of praise toward God.

APPLYING GOD'S WORD (10 minutes)
Have each person write out a personal prayer of praise to the Lord. (In Session 7 the group will discover that praise is directed toward God's character and thanksgiving toward His actions. These written prayers should focus on the character of God.)

When everyone has finished writing out their prayers, have students tell about one negative thing that has happened to them during the past month. Can they pray the prayer they just wrote in relation to their bad experience? God's character doesn't change. Challenge each student to praise God for every circumstance in his life, because it is usually the negative events that lead to spiritual growth (James 1:2-4; 2 Corinthians 12:7-10).

Close with sentence prayers of praise, honoring God for who He is.

Assignments for Next Week:
1. Complete Session7.

2. Memorize 1 Thessalonians 5:18.

3. Spend time alone with God this week focusing on praise and thanksgiving.

AFTER THE MEETING

1. Evaluate: Are the group members answering honestly, or do they give "pat" answers to questions? If you detect that they are giving the answers they know to be "right," challenge them at the next meeting to be honest with the group and with themselves.

2. If any students are not participating, are not doing their assignments, or have a negative attitude, meet with them individually this week.

SESSION 7

Give Thanks

OVERVIEW

Key Concept   An attitude of gratitude for God's gifts leads to and reflects spiritual maturity.

Memory Verse   I Thessalonians 5:18

Goals   *Individual Growth:* To develop an attitude of thankfulness for the gifts and actions of God.

                 Group Life: To express thankfulness to God for the Discipleship Group.

BEFORE THE MEETING

1. Pray for each person in the group, thanking God for the positive qualities He is building in each one's life. Ask God to give you wisdom to learn how to help each one develop a thankful heart.

2. In *Spending Time Alone with God,* complete Session 7.

3. Memorize I Thessalonians 5:18.

4. Gather materials for the meeting:
   • Bible
   • *Spending Time Alone with God*
   • Bible memory verses
   • Paper
   • *Time Alone with God Notebook*

5. Recommended option: Show the clip from *The Hiding Place* movie. Begin where Corrie and Betsie contend with the fleas and show it until they give thanks that they can discuss the guards interference. Gather the needed equipment.

THE MEETING

BUILDING THE GROUP (20 minutes)
Discuss the similarities and differences between praise and

thanksgiving. Explain that the terms are often used interchangeably, but we are making a distinction between God's characteristics (for which we praise Him) and His gifts and actions (for which we thank Him).

As a group, make a list of God's attributes for which you can praise Him. Then for each attribute, go back and make a list of gifts the Lord gives as a result of each particular characteristic. Have the group offer sentence prayers, praising God for His attribute, then thanking God for specific gifts He has given them as a result of that attribute. Use this as a way to show the difference between praise and thanksgiving.

FOCUSING ON LIFE (10 minutes)
Discuss: **Think about one person you see every day at school or work. Does he tend to be thankful? Explain your answer. Do you consider yourself a thankful person? How has this week's study helped you become a more thankful person?**

EXPLORING GOD'S WORD (30 minutes)
Allow time for group members to review their answers and comments for Session 7 in *Spending Time Alone with God*. Encourage them to ask questions and make observations. Then discuss these questions:

1. What are some things for which we can always be thankful?
(Refer to the section heading in Session 7, "Giving Thanks: Working It Out.")

2. What was Job's response when his friends tried to get him to repent for sins he had not committed? (Job 13:15) **What word in verse 15 describes Job's attitude toward God?** (hope or trust) **Does that mean Job never questioned what happened to him?**

Explain that even though tragedy had struck Job, he was still thankful to God. Job knew that no matter how bad his circumstances were, he could trust in the God whose character never changes. However, Job didn't always understand God's actions and was not afraid to ask, "Why?" Explain that God desires our honesty and we can question Him if we don't understand our circumstances.

As a commitment to develop a thankful attitude in all areas of life, quote the memory verse, 1 Thessalonians 5:18, together.

APPLYING GOD'S WORD (15 minutes)

Option 1: Ask each person to write in his *Time Alone with God Notebook*: (1) one thing he is particularly thankful for this week and one thing he has had problems being thankful for (an unpleasant person, a physical characteristic, etc.) Encourage each person to thank God for both of those things every day this week. (2) one way he will demonstrate his thankfulness for another member of the Discipleship Group (Examples: send a note, tell that person why he appreciates him, thank him for something he has done, take him to get a burger, etc.)

Option 2: Show *The Hiding Place* movie section about the fleas. Explain that the author and her sister were placed in Ravensbruck, the notorious German concentration camp, during World War II. Yet even under those horrible conditions, they learned to thank God for every circumstance – even the fleas that infested their living quarters. Later, God allowed the women to discover His purpose for those fleas, and how He had used them to accomplish His will in the midst of a hate-filled camp.

After the movie clip, have each person make a list of things he finds it hard to thank God for. Challenge everyone to begin thanking God for those things in spite of how they feel during time their alone with God this week.

Assignments for Next Week:
1. Complete Session 8.

2. Memorize 1 John 1:9.

3. Spend time alone with God every day this week asking God to develop an attitude of thankfulness in you.

4. Begin to pray for the half day of prayer during your times alone with God.

AFTER THE MEETING

1. Evaluate: Is there a student who tends to be a loner? If so, do something with him this week. Let him know you are thankful for him. Also ask one of your more mature students to get together with him this week and plan an activity that will begin building a stronger relationship.

2. Try to meet with two or three group members this week on an individual basis.

S E S S I O N   8

Live Clean

OVERVIEW

Key Concept   Confession of sins leads to forgiveness, freedom, and closeness to God.

Memory Verse   1 John 1:9

Goals   *Individual Growth:* To experience the forgiveness, freedom, and closeness to God that comes from staying current with confession of any known sins.

Group Life: To learn to confess our sins to each other.

BEFORE THE MEETING

1. Pray that the group will grasp the concept of how God's forgiveness opens the way to freedom and closeness to God.

2. In *Spending Time Alone with God,* complete Session 8.

3. Memorize 1 John 1:9.

4. Examine your own life for any unconfessed sin. Is there anyone you need to forgive? Is there anything for which you need to ask God's forgiveness? If so, claim the promise of 1 John 1:9 for yourself before the next meeting.

5. Gather materials for the meeting:
   • Bible
   • *Spending Time Alone with God*
   • Bible memory verses
   • *Time Alone with God Notebook*
   • A large nail or spike and nails for each person
   • Matches
   • Fireproof receptacle, such as a metal trash can or ashtray

THE MEETING

BUILDING THE GROUP (15 minutes)
Begin by asking how last session's discussion on thanksgiving positively impacted them. Spend a few minutes reviewing the major ideas from last week.

Then discuss: **Have you ever had a "feud" with a friend, in which both of you were so mad you wouldn't speak to each other? How did you feel after a day or two? What did it take to resolve the situation?**

Ask: **Have you ever done something that really hurt someone close to you, and even after you apologized, things just weren't the same? Did you ever regain the other person's trust? How?**

FOCUSING ON LIFE? (30 minutes)
Discuss: **Have you ever felt like you have really hurt God? How? What did you do to make things right? How did God respond? Would most people have responded in the same manner?**

Hold up a large nail or spike as you read aloud Isaiah 53:3-6. (Use a contemporary version of the Bible such as *The New Living Bible*.) Then tell each person to find a spot by himself. For a few minutes meditate on the price Jesus paid in order to forgive sins. Also ask everyone to read Psalm 103:10-12, and think about the completeness of God's forgiveness.

Reassemble the group and discuss these questions: **(1) What price did Christ pay for us to be forgiven? Was the price He paid sufficient to cover all our sins? (2) What does Psalm 103:10-12 say about removing our sins? Do you tend to remember your sins and feel guilty long after God has forgiven you?**

Explain that God has promised us forgiveness, and if we confess our sins, we are forgiven!

 EXPLORING GOD'S WORD (20 minutes)
Allow time for group members to review their answers and comments from Session 8 in *Spending Time Alone with God*. Encourage them to ask questions and make observations. Then discuss these questions:
1. What does it mean to confess your sins? (Refer to Session 8 subhead, "How Do We Confess Our Sins?".)

2. What attitude did David have when he confessed his sin (Psalm 51:17)? (His heart was broken and contrite.)

3. Psalm 51 is King David's confession. He asked God for some specific things to happen as a result of being forgiven. What are some of those requests? (Refer to Session 8 subhead, "Accept Forgiveness.") In your *Time Alone With God Notebook*, paraphrase David's prayer in your own words. Make this paraphrase your own personal prayer as you confess your sins to God.

When the group finishes, quote 1 John 1:9 together.

APPLYING GOD'S WORD (10 minutes)
Ask each student to write on a separate sheet of paper any sin(s) he has committed for which he still feels guilty. Explain that this list will remain confidential. When everyone is finished writing, have students fold their papers to keep them private. Then put all the lists into a metal wastebasket or large ashtray and burn the lists. (Make sure you can *safely* conduct this activity. You may even want to go outside for this part of the meeting.)

As the written confessions are burning, ask the group to silently confess their sins to God. Explain that God has forgiven every sin that has been confessed. However, if some of the sins involved other people, they need to make things right with those persons. If the sin was against another person in the group, encourage those involved to settle the issue before leaving the meeting.

Assignments for Next Week
1. Complete Session 9.

2. Memorize Matthew 7:7-8.

3. Spend time alone with God daily focusing on honesty in confessing your sins and God's total forgiveness through the Cross.

4. Continue to remember the upcoming half day of prayer during your daily times alone with God.

AFTER THE MEETING

1. Evaluate: Do you detect any cliques among the members of your Discipleship Group? If so, try to pair different people before and after the meetings to strengthen the weaker relationships.

2. Are all of the students keeping up with their daily times alone with God, weekly assignments, and memory verses? As you see different ones in the group this week, talk to them about their assignments. Make sure they are keeping up. Help them if they are not.

3. Begin to plan specific details for your half day of prayer (location, materials needed, transportation, etc.). Delegate one specific assignment to each person in the group so that they own this event.

SESSION 9

Pray for Yourself

OVERVIEW

Key Concept   God is a loving Father who wants us to bring our needs to Him.

Memory Verse   Matthew 7:7-8

Goals   *Individual Growth:* To discover the privilege of making our personal needs known to God and receiving His provision for them.

    Group Life: To practice petition as a group by praying specifically for the Discipleship Group.

BEFORE THE MEETING

1. Pray that each person will understand the importance of petition and the privilege of approaching God as a loving Father who wants to meet our needs.

2. In *Spending Time Alone with God*, complete Session 9.

3. Memorize Matthew 7:7-8.

4. Gather materials for the meeting:
   - Bible
   - *Spending Time Alone with God*
   - Bible memory verses
   - *Time Alone with God Notebook*

THE MEETING

BUILDING THE GROUP (15 minutes)
Discuss the following:
Describe how you viewed God when you were young. What character qualities did He have? What physical qualities? Did He ever seem like an invisible cloud or a Santa Claus?

What kinds of prayers did you pray to God at that age?

Have your prayers changed since then? How?

How has your mental image of God changed as you have grown older?

FOCUSING ON LIFE (15 minutes)
When you were a small child, who took care of your daily needs? (parents or guardians) **Did they ever intentionally keep you from having anything you really needed? Does that mean you never had to ask them for anything?** (even though loving parents want to provide for their children)

Since God already knows what we need, why is it still important to ask Him for those things? (God, our loving Father, likes for us to ask Him for things. Petition shows that we trust Him to take care of us, and it reminds us that we are not self-sufficient.)

EXPLORING GOD'S WORD (35 minutes)
Allow time for the group to review their answers and comments for Session 9 in *Spending Time Alone with God*. Encourage them to ask questions and make observations. Then discuss these questions:
1. How would your define *petition*?

2. What conditions must be met in order for our prayers to be answered? (belief that God will hear us; prayer in Jesus' name; remaining in Christ)

3. Why does God refuse our requests at times? (wrong motives, unbelief, prayers that don't agree with His character and purposes – see Session 5.)

4. What does it mean to ask "in Jesus' name"? (See the subhead, "Petition: Asking.") **Will praying in Jesus' name change the way you've prayed in the past? Why or why not?**

5. The Bible contains thousands of promises. What are some promises in Scripture that you want to ask God to become a reality in your life in the weeks to come?

APPLYING GOD'S WORD (10 minutes)
Close with prayers of petition. Ask each person to pray one specific request before the rest of the group. Ask God to meet specific needs. Then encourage everyone to pray for the Discipleship Family as a whole. List three group needs as you pray. Complete your time of prayer by quoting the memory verses, Matthew 7:7-8, together.

Before dismissing, remind your group members of the half day of prayer (which should take place after your next meeting). Assign specific responsibilities to each student (planning transportation, bringing needed materials, etc.).

Assignments for Next Week:
1. Complete Session 10.

2. Memorize 2 Corinthians 10:4-5.

3. Spend time alone with God every day asking Him to show you your real, deep needs.

4. Review the material already covered in *Spending Time Alone with God* and all the memory verses. Write down any questions you have.

AFTER THE MEETING

1. Evaluate: Can you see a difference in people in the group as they have entered into the disciplines of prayer, Bible study, and Scripture memory during the past nine weeks? If you have noticed that any topics might not be clear to the group, be prepared to discuss them during the next meeting.

2. If you are aware that any student is struggling with an issue raised during the study of *Spending Time Alone with God,* talk to him this week about his concern.

3. Send all group members an e-mail, reminding them that next week is the last meeting and to review all memory verses. Assure each one of your prayers, your friendship, and your willingness to help in any way you can.

4. Finalize your plans for the half day of prayer.

Pray for Others

OVERVIEW

Key Concept   Intercessory prayer is the greatest weapon believers have for influencing the lives of others.

Memory Verse   2 Corinthians 10:4-5

Goals   *Individual Growth:* To experience the joy of seeing God impact other people's lives as a result of intercessory prayer.

Group Life: To select group members for whom to intercede in the weeks following this last Discipleship Group meeting.

BEFORE THE MEETING

1. Pray for each person by name, asking God to give each one the desire and discipline to pray for others.

2. In *Spending Time Alone with God,* complete Session 10.

3. Memorize 2 Corinthians 10:4-5.

4. Gather materials for the meeting:
   - Bible
   - *Spending Time Alone with God*
   - Bible memory verses
   - *Time Alone with God Notebook*

THE MEETING

BUILDING THE GROUP (15 minutes)
When the group assembles, have each person report results from their prayers of petition during the week. What did they pray for? What promise did they claim? Were any prayers answered? (Keep in mind that *no* and *wait* are valid answers to prayer.)

After you have answered any questions concerning petition, ask someone to read the introduction to Session 10, down to the heading, "How Intercession Works." Ask the group: **Have you ever had experiences such as these, where you were asked for help, but didn't know what to do? What did you do?**

Spend a few minutes discussing your students' experiences. Perhaps prayer was a natural response for some of them. If so, ask if they prayed in confidence that God would take action, or if their prayer was more from desperation and lack of knowing what else to do.

Make sure all examples discussed at this time are from the past. The next section will cover *current* problems.

FOCUSING ON LIFE (10 minutes)
Discuss the following questions:
Who is a friend whose life you would like to see changed?
(Ask them to think about someone outside the group.) **What change would you like to see?** (Give up a sinful habit, become a Christian, start going to church, etc.)

Have you tried to do anything to make that person change? What have you done? What were the results?

After completing this week's study, did you pray for that person?

EXPLORING GOD'S WORD (20 minutes)
Allow time for group members to review their answers and comments from Session 10 in *Spending Time Alone with God.*
Encourage members to ask questions and make observations. Then discuss these questions:
1. Why are your prayers important in God's process of touching other people's lives? (Even if the other person doesn't pray, God will hear our intercessory prayers.)

2. What is the Holy Spirit's function in intercessory prayer? (He penetrates the life of the other person no matter where he is or what his circumstances are.)

3. How many times should you pray for someone? (See 1 Samuel 12:23.)

4. Why is it good for several people to pray for the same thing? (See Matthew 18:18-20.)

5. What are some steps to effective intercessory prayer? (Refer to the Session 10 subhead, "Steps to Powerful Intercessory Prayer.")

Recite 2 Corinthians 10:4-5 together. Remind the group that any stronghold or resistance can be destroyed through intercessory prayer.

APPLYING GOD'S WORD (30 minutes)
Ask each group to write in his *Time Alone with God Notebook* the name of the person outside the group that he would like to pray for. Then divide the group into pairs, and have each person add to his notebook the name of the person his partner is praying for. Ask everyone to pray for the those people for the next 30 days. Encourage prayer partners to check with each other at least once a week for progress reports.

Then spend a few minutes reviewing the material covered in *Spending Time Alone with God*. Use the following questions as guidelines:

(1) How has your daily time alone with God affected your life over the past 10 weeks?

(2) What have you learned from spending time in God's Word?

(3) Has the Scripture you have memorized so far helped you overcome any hard-to-handle situations?

(4) Has God answered yes to any of your recent prayers?

(5) Has He answered no, or wait? Can you understand why?

(6) Why praise God? How does praise affect how you handle problems in life?

(7) What is the difference between praise and thanksgiving? Why can we still be thankful even if we're in the midst of a struggle or tragedy?

(8) How have you experienced forgiveness through confession? What is God's promise when you confess?

(9) What have you discovered about praying for yourself?

Review the 10 memory verses from *Spending Time Alone with God* (in groups of two if time is limited).

Ask the group to pray sentence prayers expressing thanks to God for what they have learned so far, and asking God to cause each student to draw nearer to Him.

Before dismissing, issue a challenge to your group. Explain that even though they have completed *Spending Time Alone with God*, their daily times alone with God need to continue. (The Assignment section of Session 10 contains the rest of the breakdown of the Gospel of John so they can continue.) Now that they have fulfilled their 10-week commitment, encourage them to make a lifelong commitment to pursue God by spending time alone with Him each day.

One of the best ways to keep individual desire and commitment strong is to back it up with group support. Display and describe *Making Jesus Lord,* the next book in the *Moving Toward Maturity* series. Set up a meeting to organize a new Discipleship Group, and encourage each person to attend and renew his commitment to the group.

Make sure everyone knows the time and place for the half day of prayer, and what to bring. Answer any final questions students might have.

No Assignment

AFTER THE MEETING

Contact each member of the group a week or so before your first meeting for the Making Jesus Lord Discipleship Group. Encourage every person to continue his commitment to the group.

PLANNING A HALF DAY OF PRAYER

After students complete their 10-week study of *Spending Time Alone with God*, an organized half day of prayer can be a special experience as they are given the opportunity to apply everything they have learned. Set a date for this event early in the study, but don't say too much about it until you get to Session 6 (the first session on prayer).

Structure this activity to meet the needs of your specific group. Be creative. Vary the prayer times to meet the needs of the group. The outline below should get you started in the right direction. Your enthusiasm about this will influence the group. The more enthusiasm you show for this activity, the more excited your students will become.

Step #1: Orientation (10 minutes)
Meet together to express the purpose, discuss the schedule, hand out any materials you have prepared, and answer questions.

Step #2: Individual prayer (2 hours)
Have your students get alone to spend individual time with God. They should gauge their time in order to cover three major areas:
  • *Waiting on the Lord* – Realize His presence, experience cleansing, and worship Him.

  • *Praying for Others* – Intercede for others.

  • *Praying for Themselves* – Petition God openly and honestly about their own needs.

Students should vary their activities during each of these areas. They can pray a while (both aloud and silently), read the Scriptures, plan and organize, or whatever else is relevant to this special time alone with God. They should list the requests in their *Time Alone with God Notebook* so they can follow up on them in future prayer times. This is a terrific opportunity for them to put into practice everything they have learned over the last ten weeks.

Step #3 – Response (50 minutes)
Reassemble as a group and ask each person to express one specific way he drew near to God through this experience. Allow the discussion to flow from there. Pray together as a group for at least half of this time.

MATERIALS NEEDED:

Essential

Bible
Time Alone with God Notebook
Pen
Clock or watch
Scripture memory cards

Helpful

Sack lunch/beverage (or they can fast)
CD's of worship songs and a diskman
Devotional/Prayer books
School annual or newspaper to pray for their friends at school

Other Options

List of personal goals/objectives to pray about
List of personal decisions to pray over
Schedule and activities to pray about

MAKING JESUS LORD

Leader's Guide prepared by
Barry St. Clair and Sandy Larsen

Leading Your Discipleship Group

Moving Toward Maturity is a five-part discipleship training series for young people. It is designed to help them become independently dependent on Jesus Christ and then teach others to do the same. This series has four main purposes:

    1. To encourage students to passionately pursue Jesus Christ.

    2. To help young people develop strong, Christ-like character.

    3. To train young people in the "how to's" of Christian living.

    4. To move young people from the point of getting to know Jesus Christ to the point of offering Him to others.

Making Jesus Lord, the third book in the series, challenges students to yield their lives completely to the lordship of Jesus Christ. Your group will take a realistic look at Jesus' credentials for lordship, weigh the costs and benefits of submitting to Jesus' lordship, and examine their lives and make decisions that will lead to making Jesus Lord.

The other four study books in the series and related materials are described on the outside back cover of this Leader's Guide.

IMPORTANT NOTE: This Leader's Guide contains vital instructions, hints, and direction to help you lead your group most effectively. **We have placed this important information in only one place in the Leader's Guide, pages 7-11 in the *Following Jesus* section of the Leader's Guide.** Each time you begin a new book, review thoroughly the "Leading Your Discipleship Group" material. By doing so, you will sharpen your own leadership abilities. Through God's Spirit and your investment, students' lives will change.

SCRIPTURE MEMORY NOTE: Each Moving Toward Maturity book contains Bible memory verses that students memorize each week. These verses are found on the last page of each book. Since students tend to have trouble memorizing verses, your encouragement will help them succeed. The design of these books does not allow us to provide removable Scripture memory cards. Help by giving them ten small blank cards with a rubber band. Each week, when you make the assignments, have them write out the verse for the week on the card. Encourage them to carry the verses with them to review during the week. Keep extra cards in case they lose them. Helping your students succeed in memorizing Scripture is one of the greatest gifts you can give them!

INTRODUCTORY SESSION

Continuing Your Discipleship Group

OVERVIEW

Key Concept   Through the group experience and individually pursuing Jesus to understand and apply what it means to make Jesus Lord.

Goals   *Individual Growth:* To pursue Jesus' lordship in my life by accepting the responsibilities of a Discipleship Group for another 10-week experience.

Group Life: To build stronger, deeper relationships within the group.

BEFORE THE MEETING

1. Study pages 6-11 of this Leader's Guide for important background information.

2. In *Making Jesus Lord,* prepare Session 1, and put together the memory verse packet located in the back of the book.

3. Call each person who said he would come to the first meeting. Your group should consist of students who finished *Following Jesus* and *Spending Time Alone with God.* Ask everyone to bring their school and work schedules.

4. Be prepared to present the purpose of the Moving Toward Maturity series to the group. Explain the content of *Making Jesus Lord.*

5. Gather materials for the meeting:
   - Bible
   - *Making Jesus Lord*
   - 3"x 5" cards
   - Sheets of 8-1/2" x 11" paper, preferably in colors

- Pencils
- Bible memory verses
- Student materials (a copy of *Making Jesus Lord* and a *Time Alone with God Notebook* for each person)

THE MEETING

BUILDING THE GROUP (20 minutes)
As each person arrives, greet him warmly and ask him to write his name, address, e-mail address, and phone number on a 3"x 5" card in order to update his personal information (unless you already have this information from a previous Discipleship Group).

When everyone has arrived, give each person a sheet of 8-1/2"x 11" paper and ask him to draw or write a paragraph about something in his life which is very important to him. It may be a possession, another person, a life goal, a hobby or activity, anything at all – including his relationship with the Lord. (Take part in this activity yourself.) Let each person share what he has drawn or written. (You go first.)

FOCUSING ON LIFE (5 minutes)
Discuss: **What person has had the most influence on you? How and why?** (Let the group respond.) **What different does it make what kind of people influence us?** (We'll tend to become like the people who influence us, taking on their values and ways of looking at life, even their behavior.) Record the response of your group to use later in "Considering the Choice."

EXPLORING THE CHALLENGE (20 minutes)
Have a volunteer read Colossians 2:6-10. Emphasize to the group that just as they have begun their lives with Christ by faith, they must continue to live with Him by faith, trusting more and more of their lives to Him.

Review the purpose of the Moving Toward Maturity series (page 92 of this Leader's Guide). Let each student share something he learned or experienced from being in a previous Discipleship Group. Stress that the focus of the group is to grow in their relationship to Christ and to each other.

Give everyone a copy of *Making Jesus Lord* (collect their money for this book and *Time Alone with God Notebook* if you have not done so already).

Review the topics, and read the group disciplines under "Personal Commitment" (page 11). Discuss any questions students have about the group disciplines.

Also hand out copies of the *Time Alone with God Notebook*. Explain that the group will continue their daily times alone with God as they learn to make Jesus Lord of their lives. Challenge them to deepen their intimacy with Christ every day in their times alone with God. Follow the weekly assignments to read through the Gospel of Mark.

Briefly discuss the length and number of meetings (one hour to one and one-half hours per week with the group, plus individual preparation time, plus time alone with God, for the next ten weeks.) Then have everyone consult their schedules and decide on a specific time and place to meet.

CONSIDERING THE CHOICE (15 minutes)
Review the list you compiled earlier of people who have strongly influenced them. Ask the group to silently consider whether they really want Jesus Christ to be the top influence in their lives.

Challenge them to think and pray about making another 10-week commitment to the Discipleship Group. Ask them to consider seriously their decision. Encourage them not do this because everyone else is. Anyone who decides not to become a part of this particular group should let you know before the next meeting and return his unmarked copy of *Making Jesus Lord* and *Time Alone with God Notebook*. Those who choose to continue need to complete Session 1 in *Making Jesus Lord* before the next meeting.

Encourage everyone to set aside a specific time each week to complete the assignments for the next Discipleship Group meeting.

Close by praying for each person by name. Thank God for each one and ask God to give each of you the desire to make Jesus Lord of your lives.

Assignments for Next Week: Give the following assignments to those who decide to be a part of the Discipleship Group:
1. In *Making Jesus Lord,* read pages 7-10, pray over, and sign the Personal Commitment sheet (page 11).

2. Complete Session 1.

3. Put together the memory verse packet in the back of the book. (Show the group your packet to demonstrate what it looks like put together.)

4. Memorize Psalm 63:1 as part of Session 1.

5. Bring a Bible, a pen or pencil, and *Making Jesus Lord* to every meeting.

If some students have not paid you, remind the group to bring enough money next week to reimburse you for the student books (*Making Jesus Lord* and *Time Alone with God Notebook*).

Before students leave this first meeting, try to talk with them individually. See if they have any questions or problems. Let them know you care about each of them and their concerns.

AFTER THE MEETING

1. Evaluate: Did each person become involved in sharing his ideas and feelings? Are there people who need to be drawn out to participate more freely? Review "Effective Meetings," pages 10-11 of this Leader's Guide.

2. This week, and every week, begin preparing for the next session at least five days in advance. Complete Session 1 in *Making Jesus Lord,* and read through the Leader's Guide suggestions.

Get Ready...Get Set!

OVERVIEW

Key Concept Jesus Christ deserves to be your Lord.

Memory Verse Psalm 63:1

Goals *Individual Growth:* To grasp the uniqueness and greatness of Jesus which entitles Him to be Lord.

Group Life: To encourage each other to pursue Jesus as Lord of the Discipleship Group for the next ten weeks.

BEFORE THE MEETING

1. Pray for each person in the group, asking God to give each one the desire to yield himself to the lordship of Jesus.

2. In *Making Jesus Lord,* prepare Session 1, writing your personal responses to each question. This week and every week, note in the margins other observations or personal experiences that relate to the lesson, and bring them up during the group meeting.

3. Memorize Psalm 63:1.

4. Contact each person. Remind him of the meeting time and place and answer any questions. If someone has decided not to participate in this Discipleship Group, assure him that you still care for him, and express your hope that he will be able to participate in a future group.

5. Update, addresses, e-mails, and phone numbers. Make copies for each person.

6. Consider issues in your life which need to be brought under the lordship of Jesus Christ. Since all believers need to continually grow in Christ, and all of us struggle with lordship issues, then even as the leader of this Discipleship Group, you have not "arrived" spiritually. Decide how to honestly confront yourself and submit to Jesus as Lord.

7. Gather materials for the meeting:
   • Bible

- *Making Jesus Lord*
- Copies of group members' names, addresses, e-mails, and
  phone numbers (one per student)
- Bible memory verses

THE MEETING

BUILDING THE GROUP(15 minutes)
Greet each person warmly. Confirm that by each person's presence,
he is saying, "Yes, I want to be a part of this Discipleship Group."
Have everyone turn to the *Personal Commitment* sheet (page 11 in *Making
Jesus Lord*). Read it together. Then ask anyone who hasn't already done so
to sign his sheet. (Be sure to sign yours too!)

Assure your students that you are available to help them keep their commitments to this Discipleship Group. Take time for volunteers to offer
short prayers: (1) for wisdom to understand what it means to make Jesus
Lord of their lives; and (2) for courage to make Him Lord in every area of
life.

FOCUSING ON LIFE (15 minutes)
Discuss: **If someone asked you to prove that you know how to
drive a car, how would you do it?** (Show him your driver's
license; invite him to take a drive with you; get your parents or friends to
vouch for your driving ability; show him your report card proving you
passed Driver's Ed; etc. Those "credentials" prove you can drive a car.)
**What are some other things for which we like to see people's
credentials?** (You want to be sure that the doctor who's going to oper-
ate on you is a qualified M.D.; that the dentist who's going to pull your
tooth really did graduate from dental school; that your English teacher
graduated from college, etc.) **What sort of credentials could you
expect from those people?** (diplomas; other people's recommenda-
tions; your personal experience with them professionally)

Explain that when Jesus claims the right to be Lord of our lives, He shows
us His credentials. Those credentials prove His right and ability to rule
over our lives.

EXPLORING GOD'S WORD (30 minutes)
(NOTE: Each week this section is based on the work students have
done in *Making Jesus Lord*. The discussion questions are usually not
identical to those in the book, but they draw from the same Scriptures

and assignments. This technique helps students think through what they've studied rather than just parroting written answers.)

Allow time for the group to review their written responses to Session 1 in *Making Jesus Lord*. Encourage them to ask questions and make observations. Then discuss:

1. Did it surprise you to read that Jesus Christ was in on the creation of the world, and your creation in particular? What does that tell us about Him? (It shows He is God; He existed before the world was formed; He still exists now; and He is intimately concerned with our lives.)

2. According to Hebrews 4:15, Jesus struggled with all the temptations with which we struggle. With what temptations is it hard for you to imagine Jesus struggling? (Since Jesus was perfect, we may find it hard to believe He struggled with sexual temptations, the temptation to get rich quick, the temptation to harbor bitterness and resentment. Perhaps it is hardest to imagine Him struggling with the very things that trips us up most often.) **What difference does it make that He underwent all those temptations?** (He understands us; He doesn't look down on us for being tempted; we don't have to be afraid to tell Him when we struggle.)

3. What have we been given as a result of Jesus redeeming (rescuing) us? (access to God without the barrier of sin; the assurance of His love for us; and the confidence of His forgiveness; the privilege to call ourselves God's children, etc.)

4. What are some issues in your life for which we need Christ's power? (honesty, keeping relationships pure, resisting temptations, correcting bad attitudes, coping with fears, etc.) **When Jesus is truly Lord of our lives, He will be Lord over each of those issues. His power will flow through us. But it won't be power for us to use selfishly; instead He will take charge of those issues in our lives.**

Invite the group to offer their definitions of "lord" (under the subhead, "Jesus' Responsibilities as Lord" in *Making Jesus Lord*). Use the best selections from different people's definitions and create a definition for the group. Affirm everyone's efforts as they contribute.

Point out the list of specific issues that you need to submit to Jesus' lordship ("Making It Personal," Session 1) and suggest that each person in the group circle the issue or issues they struggle with the most.

 APPLYING GOD'S WORD (10 minutes)
Have the group silently reread their answers under "Desire" in
"Making It Personal." Read aloud the prayer you wrote asking God to
give you the desire to make Jesus your Lord.

Ask them to do the same. Ask if anyone struggled with signing the statement under "Decide". Let them discuss their struggle with the group.
Assure them that you will be glad to talk and pray with them about that
issue. Point out that they need to make this decision by faith, not by feelings. Assure them that even if they cannot sign the statement now, God
will work with them as they continue to settle that struggle in this
Discipleship Group. His Spirit will help them. It is better to make a carefully thought-out decision than to dash off a signature and not mean it!

Assignments for Next Week: As you give the following assignments, be
positive. Let your students know that you have faith in them and their
desire to have Christ as the Lord of their lives.

**1. Have a time alone with God each day this week, using the
Bible readings at the end of Session 1. Use the *Time Alone with
God Notebook* .**

**2. Complete Session 2 in *Making Jesus Lord*. Don't forget to learn
the memory verse.**

**3. Each day this week write what it means to make Jesus Lord of
your life in your *Time Alone with God Notebook.***

AFTER THE MEETING

1. Evaluate the meeting: Were students relaxed, or was the atmosphere
stiff? Did everyone feel free to take part? If the atmosphere was not as
you wished, jot down some possible causes and ways you can improve the
situation next week.

2. If any person expressed personal questions or problems, meet with or
call him this week.

No Pain, No Gain

OVERVIEW

Key Concept   Having Jesus as your Lord costs, but the rewards are greater than the costs.

Memory Verse   Matthew 16:24

Goals   *Individual Growth:* To identify the personal costs of making Jesus Lord, particularly with the issue of material possessions, and to appreciate the great benefits of making Jesus Lord.

    Group Life: To encourage one another to pursue Christ despite the cost.

BEFORE THE MEETING

1. Pray for your group by name, asking God to help them think clearly about the costs and the rewards of following Jesus.

2. Complete Session 2 in *Making Jesus Lord*.

3. Memorize Matthew 16:24.

4. Gather materials for the meeting.
   - Bible
   - *Making Jesus Lord*
   - Two objects (such as two wristwatches, two radios, two calculators) — one very cheap, the other noticeably more expensive.
   - Bible memory verses

5. Remember, that as a participant in the group (not only the leader), you help the group most by taking part in all group activities and discussions. Be careful not to dominate.

THE MEETING

BUILDING THE GROUP (15 minutes)
Greet each person warmly.

Ask the group to communicate any new thoughts they have had on what it means to make Jesus their Lord.

Discuss: **What are some other "lords" that people have, besides Jesus?** (money, fame, popularity, achievement in sports or school, etc.) **Why are those "lords" not as good as having Jesus as Lord?** (they won't last, don't really satisfy, can't help when your time comes to die, etc.) **When a person realizes that the false "lord" he has pursued isn't worth his devotion, what can he do?** (Turn away from that false god and turn to Jesus in faith. He is always willing to receive you.)

FOCUSING ON LIFE (10 minutes)

Show the group the two objects you brought (one cheap, the other expensive). Ask: **Which one of these is worth more?** (Let the students respond.) **What makes you think so?** (Usually we assume that if something costs more, it is better than something costing less. The higher cost reflects better workmanship, better materials, a better guarantee. It's true that many good things in life are free, and some expensive things are a rip-off, but in general, a higher price indicates higher quality.) **What does this have to do with our session this week in _Making Jesus Lord_?** (Making Jesus Lord has a high price.) **Jesus paid the price to rescue us. That's the highest price ever paid for anything. And Jesus offers the gift of Himself for free. All He asks in return is that we give Him everything.**

EXPLORING GOD'S WORD (30 minutes)

Allow time for the group to review their answers for Session 2 in _Making Jesus Lord_. Encourage them to ask questions and make observations. Then discuss these questions:

1. What makes us struggle with the high cost of having Jesus as our Lord? (fear; desire to hang on to personal ambitions; doubt that the Lord will take care of us if we give up all rights to ourselves; don't want to look like a "religious fanatic")

2. What do we find in Philippians 2:5-11 that motivates us to pay the price of following Christ? (Take time to turn to Philippians 2:5-11 and read through it. Jesus has already paid the highest price; God Himself became a human being, served sinful people, and was humiliated and killed as the lowest kind of criminal.)

3. What further motivation can we find in Galatians 2:20? (Being "crucified with Christ" is only half of the equation. Jesus living His life in us is the other half. Just as Jesus' crucifixion wasn't the end for Him, but was followed by His resurrection, so dying to ourselves is not the end; instead, He fills us with life. That's so much better than what we had before. Making Jesus Lord doesn't subtract from our lives but multiplies the quality of our lives!)

4. The Session names five "Good Deals" that we receive when Jesus is Lord of our lives. Which ones have you already experienced at some time during your walk with the Lord? (After the group responds, answer from your own experience). **Which one would you like to see more of in your life, and why?** (A person facing difficult decisions might feel a special need for "Good Deal #1." A person defeated by a sinful habit might need "Good Deal #3." Again, share a response from your own life.)

 APPLYING GOD'S WORD (15 minutes)
Say: **We have seen that because Christ was obedient to death, God exalted Him (Philippians 2:5-11). Are you willing die to yourself, your desires, hopes, and dreams in order for God to exalt you into the best life possible with Jesus? Why or why not?** (Emphasize that the decision comes down to our own individual wills. We decide who's going to be in control of our lives. Jesus will not force His lordship on us. This is a good time for you, as the leader, to briefly talk about some particular struggle you've had with making Jesus your Lord and how you decided to make the decision to follow Him.)

Under the "Making It Personal" section of Session 2, students zeroed in on the issue of material possessions. Give them the opportunity to talk about their Life Change sheets. Encourage them to be honest with group.

Ask the group to pray, thanking God for giving us a Savior who is worth the price of everything we can give to Him.

Assignments for Next Week:
1. Complete Session 3 in *Making Jesus Lord.*

2. **Continue to use the suggested Bible readings for your daily time alone with God.**

3. **Memorize 1 Peter 1:15-16. Review Psalm 63:1 and Matthew 16:24.**

AFTER THE MEETING

1. Evaluate the meeting: Did students fully understand both the costs and benefits of following Jesus?

2. Is anyone shying away from making Jesus Lord? Spend some time encouraging that person this week, either over the phone or in person.

What's the Difference?

OVERVIEW

Key Concept   Jesus is God, and because He lives in us we are very special. He is worthy of our highest commitment and devotion.

Memory Verse   1 Peter 1:15-16

Goals   *Individual Growth:* To grasp that Jesus, because He is God, and He lives in us, makes us holy.

Group Life: To agree to act holy because we are holy in the areas of dating and sexual relationships.

BEFORE THE MEETING

1. Pray for each person, particularly about their struggles in sex and dating.

2. Complete Session 3 in *Making Jesus Lord*. Even if you have been married for years and "dating" may seem like a dead issue to you, don't skip doing the Life Change sheet for yourself.

3. Memorize 1 Peter 1:15-16 and review the preceding memory verses.

4. Gather materials for the meeting:
    • Bible
    • *Making Jesus Lord*
    • Bible memory verses

THE MEETING

BUILDING THE GROUP (10 minutes)
Welcome each person warmly. If you know of some specific activities in your students' lives this week, ask about them (a test, an award, a sports event, an illness in the family, etc.).

FOCUSING ON LIFE (15 minutes)
Ask: **What do you own that has special value to you?** (Let students respond.) **Why is it special to you?** (because it's unique in some way, because of who gave it to you, because of how you acquired it, etc.) **Name a special person in your life. Why is that person spe-**

cial? (the example that person sets, special help the person has given in the past, something you have in common, etc.)

EXPLORING GOD'S WORD (35 minutes)
Have each person review Session 3 in *Making Jesus Lord*. Encourage questions or observations about the study. Then discuss:

1. **What difference does it make to you personally that God is great? Or does God's greatness seem like a far-off concept that doesn't have much to do with you personally?** (God, in His greatness, can solve any problem; He is aware of every detail of our lives. At the same time, He knows our problems and is the solution to every one of them.)

2. **Have you ever trusted in someone who failed you? What were the results and how did you feel? How do you know that you can trust God?** (His Word, the promises He has kept, His faithfulness in the lives of other people, etc.)

3. **Why does calling somebody "holy" or a "Holy Joe" sound like an insult?** (It implies that person thinks he's better than everybody else.) **What does it really mean to be holy?** (set apart and separated; pure; special) **The Bible says that God is holy** (for example, Isaiah 6:3) **and that we should also be holy** (for example, this week's memory verses, I Peter 1:15-16). **What is the difference between God's holiness and our holiness?** (God is holy in and of Himself. Read the A.W. Tozer quote under *Making Jesus Lord* subhead, "What is God Like?" (Quality #3). Then read Hebrews 10:10. Ask: **What does Jesus have to do with our holiness?** (Jesus died to bring us back to God and rid us of our sin. Without Him, we would still be devoted to our own selfish ways. Jesus rose and sent His Holy Spirit to live inside of us to make us holy.)

Point out that Jesus has made us holy by dealing with our sin on the cross and putting His Holy Spirit inside of us. Our holiness is not a fuzzy, abstract ideal but really who we are. The chart in Session 3 subtitled, "Being Set Apart" shows how we live out being holy - "putting off" and "putting on". As we do that we express who and what we already are – holy!

APPLYING GOD'S WORD (15 minutes)
Say: **God is special, the most special Person of all. And we're special to Him, so special that He gave His Son for us and set us apart. Because we're "set apart" for Him, He cares how we live. He wants to change us in those areas of our lives that don't reflect His holiness. Our Life Change sheet this week focuses on sex and dating. As you reflected on the two Scripture**

passages, **what did you discover?** (Let students respond.) Read 2 Corinthians 6:14 and discuss the issue of dating non-believers. Summarize: **God wants both partners in a marriage to be believers so together they can pursue His purposes and plans. Dating prepares us for marriage. Attitudes and actions we have in dating carry over into marriage. That means that in our relationships we date only believers and physically we remain pure.** Then read 1 Thessalonians 4:3-8. Summarize: **God has designed sex and He designed it to enjoy! He wants our sex lives to be the best. Instant gratification means less than the best. Therefore, wait until marriage. God's very best for our dating and sex life is that we don't cheat ourselves or others** (v. 6). **What will it take to get yourself in line with God's very best for your dating and sex life?**

If you have a mixed group of guys and girls, you may want to separate the sexes for the purpose of keeping the conversation as open and honest as possible.

Be sensitive to the attitude of your Discipleship Group members at this point. Are they open to a lively discussion to discover God's desires on the topic of sex and dating, or are they becoming withdrawn and uncomfortable? Leave time to pray for God's strength and guidance on this important topic.

Assignments for Next Week:
1. Complete Session 4 in *Making Jesus Lord.*

2. Memorize Hebrews 11:1. If you are having trouble memorizing the Scripture verses, find someone else in the group and work together on memorizing. You can check on and help each other.

3. Spend at least 15 minutes each day on your *Time Alone with God,* **using the Bible readings suggested at the end of Session 3 and praying.**

AFTER THE MEETING

1. Evaluate the meeting: Were students open and honest discussing sex and dating? Are they comfortable enough with each other to talk honestly about their personal lives?
2. If someone in the group is seriously involved in a relationship with a non-believer or involved sexually, look for a natural opening to discuss that relationship with him.

SESSION 4

Total Confidence

OVERVIEW

Key Concept   Because God is faithful, we can put our faith in Him.

Memory Verse   Hebrews 11:1

Goals   *Individual Growth*: Only by faith can we experience God's maximum potential in our lives.

Group Life: To encourage one another to put our faith into action.

BEFORE THE MEETING

1. Pray for each person and for your own sensitivity to each person's needs and struggles.

2. Complete Session 4 in *Making Jesus Lord*.

3. Think of an example from your life when you put your faith into action. Prepare to tell the group about your experience.

4. Meet with any person who needs special attention.

5. Memorize Hebrew 11:1.

6. Gather materials for the meeting:
   - Bible
   - *Making Jesus Lord*
   - Bible memory verses

THE MEETING

BUILDING THE GROUP (10 minutes)
Say: **Name one thing you used to believe in but later found out wasn't true?** (Santa Claus, the tooth fairy, the Easter bunny, etc.) **How did you find out you were wrong?** (Most likely the belief was put to the test and it failed. For example, a person may have spied on Santa Claus and discovered his dad was Santa.)

FOCUSING ON LIFE (10 minutes)

Select two volunteers – one large, strong person and a smaller one. Have the smaller person stand about three or four feet in front of the larger one (facing the same direction.) On your signal, the front (smaller) person should close his eyes and fall backward if he has faith that the other person will catch him.

After the person has fallen backward (or chosen not to fall backward), discuss the parallels of this simple exercise with your group's faith in God. (The smaller person couldn't see the larger person who would keep him from falling; he had to believe that the other person physically could catch him; he had to believe that the other person *would* catch him, etc.)

Summarize: **(Name of smaller student) could have verbally expressed his faith in (name of larger student) all day long. But he couldn't put his faith into action until he fell backward and allowed himself to be caught.**

EXPLORING GOD'S WORD (35 minutes)

Have students turn to Session 4 in *Making Jesus Lord* and review their written responses. Encourage them to ask questions or make comments. Then discuss:

1. Some people say, "It doesn't matter what you believe, as long as you believe." What's wrong with that statement? (Faith only makes sense when it has a trustworthy object.)

2. What if we say we believe in God, but He really doesn't exist? What would be different? (no light, color, people, oceans, mountains, etc.)

3. Because God does exist, what makes Him trustworthy? (His character, His faithfulness, etc.) **Is there a time you deliberately decided to trust God, you put your faith into action, even if you were scared?** (Ask students to give examples. Relate an example of your own, as well.)

4. Read Luke 16:10. Ask: **What does the verse tell us about trusting God in big and small situations?** (The way we respond to God in life's small situations is how we'll respond in more difficult ones.) **What's an example of a small situation where it's easy not to trust God?**

(covering up with a little lie; taking advantage of a teacher's grading error; sneaking around a parental rule, etc.)

4. Define "faith" from Hebrews 11:1; Hebrews 11:6, and Mark 11:24. Let's come up with a group definition. (Faith is confidence in God's existence, His care for us, and our trust in God that causes us to take action.)

APPLYING GOD'S WORD (15 minutes)
Ask: **With what issue do you have the biggest struggle to trust God?** (Let students privately write their answers.) **What one small step can you take to begin to trust God with that issue? Remember Luke 16:10 – if you're faithful in small things, you'll be faithful in the big things.** (Give students time to write their answers and then talk about what they wrote.)

Pray together in pairs. Ask them to honestly express their struggle to God, asking Him to give them faith to trust Him. Encourage each one to pray and have their partner pray for them.

To close, stay in pairs and have each student discuss his Life Change sheet on "Friendship" with his partner.

Assignments for Next Week: As you give the following assignments, point out that the next session is #5, which means you'll be halfway through *Making Jesus Lord*!
1. Complete Session 5 in *Making Jesus Lord*, memorize John 14:21, and continue spending time alone with God using the daily Bible readings.

2. Think about your growth in this first half of the Discipleship Group. What changes have occurred in you?

AFTER THE MEETING

1. Evaluate the meeting: Does the group talk? Do you dominate the conversation, or do they do most of the talking?

2. Are they honest about what they say or are they giving "pat answers"? Do they pray openly, honest, and sincerely?

S E S S I O N 5

For Real

OVERVIEW

Key Concept   Jesus is God and deserves our obedience.

Memory Verse   John 14:21

Goals   *Individual Growth:* To recognize that because Jesus is God, obeying Him is the key to letting Jesus be the Lord of our lives.

                 Group Life: To encourage one another to obey Christ when that is hard to do.

BEFORE THE MEETING

1. Pray that God will increase the desire of your group to obey Him in specific decisions.

2. Complete Session 5 in *Making Jesus Lord.*

3. Memorize John 14:21.

4. Evaluate the progress of your group during the first half of this Discipleship Group. Note changes in your own attitudes or actions, new challenges God has shown you, areas of spiritual struggle He has revealed to you.

5. Gather materials for the meeting:
   • Bible
   • *Making Jesus Lord*
   • Bible memory verses

THE MEETING

BUILDING THE GROUP (10 minutes)

As group members arrive, get them into groups of three or four and plan a short skit that will demonstrate the negative results of a rumor. Each skit needs to include an encounter with the person being talked about. Ideas to suggest if they can't think of anything:

• One student tells another student that his history teacher is gay.

• The word spreads in the locker room that the football quarterback is taking steroids.

• A jealous girl tries to convince everyone at the lunch table that the homecoming queen works as a waitress at a sleazy bar down town.

• After an unpopular guy scores high on his SAT, several students decide to tell everyone he cheated.

As the groups present their skits, ask them to look for motives that cause rumors to get started. Also watch for reactions of the "rumorees" when they hear what is being said about them.

FOCUSING ON LIFE (10 minutes)
Ask: **Have you ever been the subject of a rumor?** (Ask students to respond.) **How did you feel when you realized people were spreading untrue statements about you?** (response)

Many people say that Jesus Christ wasn't really who He said He was. Who do they say He was? (a great teacher, but not the Son of God; a fake and a phony who tricked a lot of people; an ordinary religious person whose followers exaggerated His deeds; etc.)

EXPLORING GOD'S WORD (35 minutes)
Encourage students to look over Session 5 in *Making Jesus Lord* and ask questions or make responses. Discuss:

1. Which of the fulfilled prophecies under "Truth #1" is most impressive to you, and why?

2. Why is it impossible to say that Jesus was a great moral teacher, but not the Son of God? (He claimed to be the Son of God, forgive sins, do miracles, and rise from the dead. So if He couldn't or didn't do those things, He's the world's biggest liar – hardly a great moral teacher!)

3. Do you find Jesus' resurrection difficult or easy to believe?

Why? (Though many have heard it taught all their lives, the Resurrection is actually an amazing and revolutionary fact. It's hard to grasp how amazing it really is.)

4. Jesus is the greatest person who ever lived. Yet He was a perfect example of humility in His obedience to His heavenly Father. Have students read John 6:38 and Matthew 26:36-46. Then have them give their definitions of obedience (Session 5 subhead, "Trust and Obey").

5. What are some results of obeying God? (Some results are listed in Session 5. Ask students to suggest others.)

6. As you read the story of Barry St. Clair's struggle with whether basketball or God was going to come first in his life, ask yourself what issues you would have struggled with in that situation. (Possibilities: Is putting God first really worth it? Have I made a big mistake by becoming a believer? Can I be happy not playing basketball? Does God really love me if He's going to take basketball away from me? Will He give basketball back to me if I give it up?) **Have you ever asked similar questions when deciding whether or not to obey God?** (Let students be honest by expressing their thoughts and share from your own experience also.)

Summarize: **In one way or another, God always rewards obedience!**

Ask your group to talk about their responses to the Life Change sheet "Obedience to Parents." Discuss the similarities between obeying Christ and obeying parents.

 APPLYING GOD'S WORD (15 minutes)
Pick one of the two options for this part of your Discipleship Group meeting time. If you have time, do both options.

Option #1: Discuss and pray over students' answers to, "Name one issue in your life where it is really tough for you to obey Jesus Christ."

Option #2: Since you are now halfway through this Discipleship Group, spend some time reflecting on changes God has made in people's lives through what they have learned. Thank God for the changes, and pray for the courage to continue to trust God and obey Him.

Assignments for Next Week: Give the following assignments:

1. Complete Session 6 in *Making Jesus Lord*.

2. Memorize Philippians 2:5.

3. Continue to have your daily time alone with God.

AFTER THE MEETING

1. Evaluate the meeting: Do students understand that obeying God is costly, but will bring rewards?

2. Are some students lagging in their preparation of the sessions or in other disciplines of the Discipleship Group? Give special encouragement and help to any who need it.

3. If student enthusiasm seems to be lagging, analyze your meetings. Are you feeling burned out? Are your students overcommitted? Are they coming to the meetings prepared? Are they engaging in the discussion seriously? Are you spending personal time with students outside the group? Perhaps you need to add something to the meetings that will provide variety. List some possible suggestions that might increase motivation (an outing, an activity, a different place to meet, refreshments, a change in the format, etc.).

Go for It!

OVERVIEW

Key Concept   Jesus' servant attitude is to be our attitude.

Memory Verse   Philippians 2:5

Goals   *Individual Growth:* To become servants like Jesus was a servant.

                  Group Life: To learn to serve each other in the Discipleship Group as well as to serve people outside the group.

BEFORE THE MEETING

1. Pray for each person by name. Ask God to give you an opportunity to serve each student in some special way.

2. Complete Session 6 in *Making Jesus Lord.*

3. Memorize Philippians 2:5.

4. Gather materials for the meeting:
   - Bible
   - *Making Jesus Lord*
   - Bible memory verses
   - 3"x 5" cards

THE MEETING

BUILDING THE GROUP (15 minutes)
Ask: **What's the kindest act anyone ever did for you?** (Let students respond.) **In what way was that person a servant to you?** (met your need; helped you; put your needs above his own; considered you more important than he was, etc.)

FOCUSING ON LIFE (10 minutes)
Ask: **What's the kindest act you've ever done for another person? How did that make you feel? Does it feel good to be a servant?** (Not always; it means giving up personal convenience and desires to put somebody else first. But it also provides a sense of satisfaction.)

Would you rather be a servant or a master? (Encourage students to respond honestly. Don't comment on their perspective at this point.)

EXPLORING GOD'S WORD (30 minutes)
Ask students to look over Session 6. Let them ask questions or make comments. Discuss:

1. Can we control our attitudes or not? (Some basic attitudes may have been instilled in us through our upbringing and through events while growing up. But ultimately we determine our attitudes.) **How do we know?** (Everyone has experienced some willful change of attitude; and God wouldn't tell us what attitudes to have unless we could decide to have them.)

2. Even though Jesus was God, He was still a human being. What selfish attitudes might He have chosen while He lived on earth? (pride about the miracles He could do; self-righteousness because He was sinless; snobbishness because He was special; ambition to be the world's greatest religious leader; etc.) **What attitude did He choose?** (the attitude of a servant)

3. This week's Session showed us that having Jesus' attitude will mean giving up our selfish ambitions and our rights. How did you react to that possibility? (Let students respond.)

4. How does Philippians 2:1-11 guide in our decision to become a servant? (Jesus, as God, chose to serve. Because Jesus lives in us, we can choose to become a servant too.)

5. From Jesus' life, what examples do we have that He served people? (feeding them, healing them, teaching them—often when He was exhausted and wanted to get away from the crowds, etc.) **Did Jesus show preference for serving a certain kind of person—rich people or nice people, for example?** (No. He served lepers and synagogue rulers, wealthy people and poor people, people of all ages, Jews and Gentiles, women and men.)

6. Why is it easier for us to serve some people rather than others? (Some people express gratitude for what we do; others don't. Also, it's often easier to serve people we know and like rather than strangers or enemies.) **Why are some people difficult to serve?** (they don't say thank you; they act like they don't really need our help; we dislike them and don't want to lower ourselves to serve them; they already act like they're better than we are; etc.) **What kind of people does Jesus want us to serve?** (Everyone who needs our help gets served.)

7. What was Jesus' ultimate act of service? (Look at Philippians 2:8 and Mark 10:45 to see that He gave His life for us.) **Did He want to die?** (He certainly did not. In the Garden of Gethsemane, He begged His Father to spare Him.) (See Matthew 26:36-46, a Scripture from last week's study on obedience.) **However, He put His own feelings aside to do His Father's will.** (See Matthew 26:39, 42-44 and John 6:38.) **Who did Jesus serve by dying on the cross?** (every person who has ever lived — both those who appreciate and receive his sacrifice, and those who don't)

APPLYING GOD'S WORD (10 minutes)
Have students think about somebody that they would prefer not to serve. Then pass out the 3"x 5" cards and ask them to write that person's name on one side and why they do not want to serve that person. On the other side, have them write a specific action they can do to serve that person. (This will probably not be a popular assignment.) Emphasize that the proposed acts of service should not be big, showy, phony things. They can be as simple as praying for the person. The other person doesn't even have to know who served him or how he was served. (Be sure you fill out a card!)

Discuss the attitudes your students have toward serving people they don't particularly like. Use the comments of your group to lead into a discussion of this week's Life Change sheet about attitudes. Have the group look for inconsistencies between what they wrote and how they actually feel.

Pray in twos about having the attitude of a servant toward each other. Encourage the group to think of one way they can serve one other person in the group and one person outside the group this week.

Assignments for Next Week:
1. Complete Session 7 in *Making Jesus Lord*, including memorizing Ephesians 5:18 and continuing the daily Bible readings in Mark.

2. Complete the act of service for the person whose name you wrote on the card. (Assure students you're going to do yours!)

AFTER THE MEETING

1. Evaluate the meeting: Did students feel hopeful about God's help in becoming a servant, or did they react negatively to the idea?
2. The group will learn much about being servants by seeing a servant attitude in you. What special things can you do to serve your students this week?

S E S S I O N   7

Turn Him Loose

OVERVIEW

Key Concept   Because you have received Christ, the Holy Spirit lives in you and gives you the power to live like Christ.

Memory Verse   Ephesians 5:18

Goals   *Individual Growth:* To release the Holy Spirit in each person so He can control every thought, attitude, and action.

Group Life: To become "one" in the Spirit as a group.

BEFORE THE MEETING

1. Pray for each person in your group individually. Ask God to prompt them to carry out their acts of service this week.

2. Make sure you do your own service project!

3. Complete Session 7 in *Making Jesus Lord*.

4. Memorize Ephesians 5:18.

5. Gather materials for the meeting:
   • Bible
   • *Making Jesus Lord*
   • Bible memory verses

THE MEETING

BUILDING THE GROUP (10 minutes)
Ask: **What good experiences did you have serving others this week? What experiences did you have that were difficult?**

(Let the group tell their stories, then tell about your own experience.)

FOCUSING ON LIFE (15 minutes)

Emphasize that serving people we don't care for – and for that matter, any act of serving – is motivated by God working in us and through us by the Holy Spirit.

Discuss: **When you think of the Holy Spirit, how do you imagine Him?** (maybe a ghost, an indistinct shapeless fog, an invisible power like magnetism, etc.) **It's easy to picture Jesus Christ because He was a man and we've seen so many pictures of Him — even though most are inaccurate. And it's possible to imagine God the Father because in our childhood we got impressions of what He must look like – our own fathers or an "old man with a long beard" — even though those pictures are inaccurate too. Probably for many of us, our image of the Holy Spirit is most vague.**

Jesus compares the Holy Sprit to wind (John 3:8). What do you think He meant by that? (neither can be seen, but their effects are apparent; they go everywhere freely and there is something mysterious, unpredictable, and wild about their actions)

EXPLORING GOD'S WORD (30 minutes)

Encourage the group to look over Session 7 in *Making Jesus Lord* and ask questions or make comments. Then discuss:

1. Did it surprise you to learn that Jesus was filled with the Holy Spirit? What does that say about our need to be filled with the Holy Spirit? (If even Jesus did not depend on Himself but drew on God's power, we certainly need to do the same.)

2. Were you aware that it was the Holy Sprit who drew you to Christ? (Some people have dramatic experiences of the Holy Spirit dealing with them to bring them to Christ. Others are gently nudged and may not realize that the Spirit brought them to Christ. Others have believed since childhood and can't pinpoint an exact time of conversion. But whether or not they are aware of the work of the Holy Sprit, He is the One who drew them to Christ.)

3. Look again at your answers to "Power Fact #6" and "Power Fact #7." They compose quite a list of ways the Holy Spirit works in us and for us since we follow Jesus! Draw a circle around the ones you're particularly aware of in your experiences

as a Christian. (discuss) **Draw a square around the ones you don't understand or don't think you have experienced yet.** (Discuss their thoughts about the ones they put circles and squares around.) Point out: **In all that the Spirit does, He desires to make people more aware of Jesus.**

4. What keeps us from being filled with the Holy Spirit? (Let the group discuss this.)

5. If the Holy Spirit lives in us, why do you think we don't always feel His presence? (Having continual "tingly" feelings is not what the Holy Spirit is about. He does withdraw His sense of presence when we disobey Him. Often, we are the ones who withdraw from Him.)

APPLYING GOD'S WORD (15 minutes)

Allow time for students to discuss their answers in this section after the prayer time. Discuss the Life Change sheet on "Habits", asking your group how the Holy Spirit can change their bad habits.

As a group, pray through the steps of being filled with the Spirit. (See subhead, "The Power Pact".)

Assignments for Next Week:
1. Complete Session 8 in *Making Jesus Lord*. Memorize Galatians 5:16 and continue having your daily time alone with God.

2. If you did not do your act of service during the past week, do it this week. If you did, try it again this next week.

AFTER THE MEETING

1. Evaluate the meeting: Do you find yourself giving answers to discussion questions before students have had much time to consider their answers? Don't be afraid of silence after you ask a question; students need time to think about their responses.

2. Are there any students who are reluctant to relate to you and the group? Make a special effort to contact them this week and talk about it honestly.

S E S S I O N   8

Get In Shape!

OVERVIEW

Key Concept   Overcome the hindrances to following Jesus through the presence of the Holy Spirit.

Memory Verse   Galatians 5:16

Goals   *Individual Growth:* To recognize specific hindrances to following Christ, confess them, and continue to walk in the Sprit.

                  Group Life: To encourage each other to honestly identify and deal with personal hindrances to following Christ.

BEFORE THE MEETING

1. Pray for each student's enlightenment as he works on this week's Session. Often we don't recognize the issues that hinder us from following Christ.

2. Complete Session 8 in *Making Jesus Lord*.

3. Memorize Galatians 5:16.

4. Gather materials for the meeting:
   • Bible
   • *Making Jesus Lord*
   • Bible memory verses
   • Toy man such as a soldier or cowboy (not a superhero type). Tie him up with string, small lead weights, and anything else that would hinder him from moving

THE MEETING

BUILDING THE GROUP (15 minutes)
Use this time to evaluate each person's consistency in his daily time alone with God. Discuss any questions, problems, or issues students

need to discuss. What difficulties are they experiencing? What are they doing to overcome those difficulties? What have they discovered? What positive experiences have they had in meeting with God.

FOCUSING ON LIFE (10 minutes)
Show the group the "tied-up" toy man. Say something like: **This is Jim. He wants God to use him to influence people at school for Christ. But as you can see, he has a few problems to overcome before he can accomplish his goal. What would you advise him to do?**

Let a student untangle the man. (It could take some doing if you've tied him up tightly! Cut him loose if necessary.) Ask: **How is that toy man like us?** (We get tied up, hindered by a variety of problems. We, too, must "cut loose" from those hindrances.)

(Option: You may wish to adapt this exercise involving a good-natured student. Wrap him in toilet paper for comic effect, or tie him with fishing line to show that many of our hindrances are barely visible yet strongly binding. Be creative!)

EXPLORING GOD'S WORD (35 minutes)
Encourage students to look over Session 8 and ask questions or make comments. Discuss:
1. Our toy man (or volunteer) has no trouble figuring out what his hindrances are. We can easily see and feel ropes and weights. However, seeing the spiritual hindrances is not so easy. (We can be deceived by Satan or we can kid ourselves. We can choose to ignore or rationalize hindrances.)

2. Is it possible to avoid the temptation of the hindrances listed in this week's session? (We would almost have to become hermits in order to avoid them. Even then, many would pursue us — Satan can find us anywhere we go. It's not the temptations that cause the problems. Temptations are all around us all the time. It's how we respond to the temptations. If we let them, the temptations that can destroy us also can strengthen us in our walk with God.)

3. What do all the hindrances have in common? (They prevent us from having the closeness with God that He desires.) Have each student examine his list of hindrances to see how selfishness rather than Christ motivates him. Be sure to divulge hindrances from your own list.

Explain that God wants us to respond to the hindrances that bind us by relaxing, letting Him work, and obeying what He tells us to do.

4. When you become aware of a hindrance in your life, what can you do to get back into walking in the Spirit? (Acknowledge the hindrance and admit your sin; confess it and consciously decide to put it off; accept Christ's forgiveness; accept the Spirit's filling once again.)

APPLYING GOD'S WORD (10 minutes)
Break into pairs, discuss this week's Life Change sheet, and have each person pray for the other one, that each of them will relax in knowing that his life is in God's hands and will allow the Holy Spirit to make any needed changes. (This is a good place for you, as the group's leader, to set an example of honesty about your own temptations.) Assure the group that you are available to talk and pray with them as they struggle with temptation. Encourage the group to pray for each other as well. Ask them if they would like to have a partner that will ask them how they are doing in their most difficult hindrance each week.

Assignments for Next Week:
1. Complete Session 9 in *Making Jesus Lord*.

2. Memorize Colossians 3:1.

3. Remain faithful in your daily time alone with God.

AFTER THE MEETING

1. Evaluate the meeting: Do students freely admit they are tempted, or do some still feel it necessary to hide their hindrances and put on a show of spirituality?

2. Do you see positive changes in students' lives as a result of your time together as a Discipleship Group? Make a list of the changes you see.

3. Does anyone feel put down because of struggling with a hindrance? If so, reassure him that he is normal, that God loves him, and that you love him.

4. If any of the students struggle with an issue that is causing dysfunction or emotional problems, help that student meet with a pastor or counselor.

SESSION 9

Changed and Rearranged

OVERVIEW

Key Concept   Christ renews our minds and changes our habits when we cooperate with Him.

Memory Verse   Colossians 3:1

Goals   *Individual Growth:* To exchange my life for Christ's life.

Group Life: To see each other as changed by Christ and to respond to each other accordingly.

BEFORE THE MEETING

1. Pray for each of your students' thought lives. Ask God to make each one aware of thoughts that are destructive and need to be renewed.

2. Complete Session 9 in *Making Jesus Lord*.

3. Memorize Colossians 3:1.

4. Gather materials for the meeting:
   - Bible
   - *Making Jesus Lord*
   - Two T-shirts: one dirty and sweaty, the other one new
   - Bible memory verses

THE MEETING

BUILDING THE GROUP (10 minutes)
Since this is the next-to-last meeting of your Discipleship Group, express your appreciation for the group and for how you see each one progressing.

FOCUSING ON LIFE (10 minutes)
Display the dirty T-shirt by wearing it. Say: **Suppose I want to convince you that I'm a clean person. The problem is that**

every single day you see me wearing this same dirty T-shirt. I
never change to a clean one; I never take a shower. What would
you advise me to do? (Take off the shirt and get cleaned up!)

Now put on the clean T-shirt (if decency allows!) and say: **OK, so I go
out and buy this nice new T-shirt. It's mine to wear. But instead
of putting it on, I hang it in the closet and continue to wear my
old, dirty, smelly shirt. What would you advise me to do?** (Put on
the new shirt.)

Discuss: **How do these two t-shirts illustrate the way Christ
changes us?** (He exchanges His life for our lives. Our job is to
consciously take off the "smelly" stuff in us, and put on the new, clean
thoughts, attitudes, and actions which the Holy Spirit makes possible
inside of us.)

EXPLORING GOD'S WORD (35 minutes)

Ask students to look over Session 9. Give them the opportunity to
ask questions and make comments. Then discuss:

1. **Can you think of one way you have specifically changed since
you became a Christian?** Let the group respond, and then get a little
more specific: **Can you think of one way God has helped you
change an attitude or a way of behaving in, say, the past couple
of months?** (Share your own experience of how God has changed you
after the students express their experiences.)

2. **But what if changes are not obvious in our lives? What if
nothing seems to be happening? Does that mean nothing is
changing?** (We must take God at His Word. He has made our hearts
new and is working in us even when we can't see it or feel it. At the same
time we can bring our thoughts, attitudes, and actions to God asking Him
to bring them into line with our new selves – who we are in Christ.)

3. **We are commanded to set our *hearts* on "things above"**
(Colossians 3:1) **and to set our *minds* on "things above"** (Colossians
3:2). **What's the difference between the two?** ("Heart" indicates our
deepest affections, desires, and attitudes. "Mind" indicates our conscious
and unconscious thoughts.) **Since we are told to "set" both our
hearts and minds on God, we can make a decision and take
action to do that. We can't always control what pops into our**

"radar screen", but we can decide whether or not to let it remain there.

4. Ask volunteers to define *renewal*. (A simple definition is "to be made new.") Then compare Ephesians 4:20-24 with Romans 12:2. Ask: **Who does the renewing?** (God. Notice that these passages don't tell us to renew ourselves, but to be made new.) **What is our part in being renewed?** (putting off negative thoughts, attitudes and actions; putting on Christ's thoughts, attitudes, and actions) Explain: **Renewal requires a conscious decision on our part. It begins with an understanding of what Christ's thoughts, attitudes, and actions are, through Bible study and prayer, and results in surrendering our thoughts, attitudes, and actions to Him every day.**

5. Ask the group to describe some of the thoughts they need to "put off." It's always helpful to know that others struggle with the same (or similar) problems. Honest group interaction can let each one know that he is not alone in the process of changing and rearranging.

6. In the illustration of how sin "hooks" us, what's the first opportunity sin has to get us? (our thoughts) **What's the best place to cut sin short?** (our thoughts) Summarize: **It often seems Satan knows our weaknesses and knows exactly which "lure" to use. We each have particular "enticements" we must guard against. What is yours?**

7. Look at the Christ-like qualities in Colossians 3:12-17. How does love bind them all together, as verse 14 says? (All those Christ-like qualities depend on grasping God's love for us and pursuing our love for Him and for other people.)

8. Last week's Life Change sheet dealt with temptation. This week we address our thought life. How are the two topics related? (If we put Philippians 4:8 into practice and let Christ control our thoughts, we are less likely to yield to temptation in our attitudes and actions.) After discussing the Life Change sheet, move on to related questions under Session 9 subhead, "Putting On." Talk about this thoroughly. Go over each point. Memorize together and repeat out loud several times: "I am dead to myself. I am alive to Christ. My life is hidden with Christ in God."

APPLYING GOD'S WORD (15 minutes)

Have the group spend time in silent meditation imagining themselves "in Christ." They may use any mental images that will help them "place" themselves in Him. Ask them to think of themselves as protected and enveloped by Him, so that nothing can touch them without His permission. After silent meditation and prayer, ask students to voice prayers of trust "in Christ" and thanks for their new life "in Christ".

Assignments for Next Week: Before you give the following assignments, remind students that next week is the final week of this Discipleship Group. Let them know that you will begin the next meeting with a special time of praise to God for what He has done during this study. Be positive about each person's progress and let each one know you look forward to meeting with him next week.

1. Complete Session 10 in *Making Jesus Lord*.

2. Memorize Romans 12:1-2.

3. Continue having your daily time alone with God.

4. Write down some specific ways that Jesus has become Lord of your life through this Discipleship Group.

AFTER THE MEETING

1. Evaluate the meeting: Did students grasp that they are new people in Christ even though they don't always feel like it?

2. Are there any loose ends to tie up with the students? Misunderstandings, lack of communication, payment for books, etc.? Do your best to complete these issues before the next meeting.

SESSION 10

Who Owns You?

OVERVIEW

Key Concept Jesus owns our lives and has the right to ask us to do whatever He knows is best for us.

Memory Verses Romans 12:1-2

Goals *Individual Growth:* To recognize Jesus' total ownership of each person's life.

Group Life: To praise God together for what He has done during this ten weeks.

BEFORE THE MEETING

1. Pray for each person in the group. Thank God for the opportunity to know each one. Pray for the continued growth in Christ for each person after this study ends.

2. Complete Session 10 in *Making Jesus Lord*.

3. Memorize Romans 12:1-2.

4. Write out the life changes that you can see in you and your students during these ten weeks.

5. Gather materials for the meeting:
   - Bible
   - *Making Jesus Lord*
   - A trophy, any type (but not a "joke" type)
   - Bible memory verses

THE MEETING

BUILDING THE GROUP (10 minutes)
Welcome each person warmly. Say some specific words of appreciation for each person. (You will spend more time building up one another at the end of this session.)

FOCUSING ON LIFE (10 minutes)
Show the group a trophy. Read the name on it and what it was awarded for. Ask: **What does this trophy tell you about (name of person/team)?**

If we're God's trophies, as we learned this week, what does that tell us about God? (He goes to great effort to win us and make us His own, and we're very valuable to Him.)

EXPLORING GOD'S WORD (30 minutes)
Ask students to look over Session 10 in *Making Jesus Lord*, make comments, and ask questions. Discuss:

1. Are there any limitations on that "blank check" Jesus gives you? (He wants to give us everything that is good for us. He will provide for all of our needs and many of our wants. He desires to give us life and give it abundantly.)

2. Does the thought of giving Jesus a "blank sheet" scare you? (We can't predict what He will bring into our lives — tests, difficulties, responsibilities, or joys and opportunities.) **What makes giving our "blank sheet" to Christ less scary?** (The more we trust Him, the more He proves Himself trustworthy, and the more we discover He has our best interests at heart.)

3. Ask students to give their definitions of a "living sacrifice." Ask: What's the significance of our being a sacrifice that is still "living"? (We don't just choose God's will once and then "die." Daily we make choices to die to ourselves and to live for Christ.)

4. Review your discussions of the last session on exchanging your life. (God renews us through the Holy Spirit. We cooperate with him by putting off old thoughts, attitudes, and actions and putting on new thoughts, attitudes, and actions.) Ask: **How has your life been renewed during these past 10 weeks?** (Discuss.) **Where do you still need renewing?** (Let students discuss this.)

5. Ask each student to review the Life Change sheets and pick out the one in which he thinks he needs the most help. Ask them to offer that sheet to God in prayer asking the Holy Spirit to change them specifically in that area. Encourage them to continue the life-changing process on their own after the group is over.

APPLYING GOD'S WORD (20 minutes)
Ask the students to talk about specific ways Jesus has become Lord of their lives. Give your own story also.

Spend some time in offering praise and prayers of thanksgiving for everything God has done during the past ten weeks. Close by having each person express the one specific thing from *Making Jesus Lord* that has meant the most to him, or, perhaps, the one person who has done the most to help him make Jesus the Lord of his life. Also take time to encourage students to participate in the next Discipleship Group, using Book 4 in the Moving Toward Maturity series, *Giving Away Your Faith.*

Try to talk with each person before he leaves. Thank each one for his faithfulness to the group and to the Lord. Express your confidence in each one, that he will continue making Jesus Lord.

No Assignment

AFTER THE MEETING

Contact each person in the group a week or so before beginning the next book, *Giving Away Your Faith.* Encourage every person to continue with the group.

NOTES

GIVING AWAY YOUR FAITH

Leader's Guide prepared by
Barry St. Clair and Sandy Larsen

Leading Your Discipleship Group

Moving Toward Maturity is a five-part discipleship training series for young people. It is designed to help them become independently dependent on Jesus Christ and then teach others to do the same. This series has four main purposes:

> 1. To encourage students to passionately pursue Jesus Christ.
> 2. To help young people develop strong, Christ-like character.
> 3. To train young people in the "how to's" of Christian living.
> 4. To move young people from the point of getting to know Jesus Christ to the point of offering Him to others.

Giving Away Your Faith, the fourth book in the series, will challenge your students to share their faith with others. Your group members will examine the needs of people, confront their fears, and learn how to relate Jesus Christ to their friends.

The other four study books in the series and related materials are described on the outside back cover of this Leader's Guide.

IMPORTANT NOTE: This Leader's Guide contains vital instructions, hints, and direction to help you lead your group most effectively. **We have placed this important information in only one place in the Leader's Guide, pages 7-11 in the *Following Jesus* section of the Leader's Guide.** Each time you begin a new book, review thoroughly the "Leading Your Discipleship Group" material. By doing so, you will sharpen your own leadership abilities. Through God's Spirit and your investment, students' lives will change.

SCRIPTURE MEMORY NOTE: Each Moving Toward Maturity book contains Bible memory verses that students memorize each week. These verses are found on the last page of each book. Since students tend to have trouble memorizing verses, your encouragement will help them succeed. The design of these books does not allow us to provide removable Scripture memory cards. Help by giving them ten small blank cards with a rubber band. Each week, when you make the assignments, have them write out the verse for the week on the card. Encourage them to carry the verses with them to review during the week. Keep extra cards in case they lose them. Helping your students succeed in memorizing Scripture is one of the greatest gifts you can give them!

I N T R O D U C T O R Y   S E S S I O N

Continuing Your Discipleship Group

OVERVIEW

Key Concept To benefit most from a group study of *Giving Away Your Faith*, we must commit ourselves to the disciplines of a Discipleship Group and to intentionally communicate our faith.

Goals *Individual growth:* To accept the responsibilities and commitments of a Discipleship Group for another 10-week period.

Group Life: To experience greater depth and stronger relationships within the group in the fourth Discipleship Group experience.

BEFORE THE MEETING

1. Study pages 6-11 of this Leader's Guide for important background information.

2. In *Giving Away Your Faith*, study pages 1-11, and put together the Bible verse packet in the back of the book.

3. Call each person who said he would come to the first meeting. Your group should consist of students who have been through *Following Jesus, Spending Time Alone With God,* and *Making Jesus Lord*. Ask everyone to bring their school and work schedules.

4. Be prepared to present the purpose and format of the Moving Toward Maturity series to the group and the purpose of these sessions.

5. Pray for each person in the Discipleship Group. Ask God to give each one compassion for the people you will encounter in giving away your faith.

6. Gather materials for the meeting:
    • Bible
    • *Giving Away Your Faith*

- Post-It® Notes
- 3"x 5" cards
- Pencils
- Bible memory verses
- Student materials (a copy of *Giving Away Your Faith* and a *Time Alone with God Notebook* for each person)

THE MEETING

BUILDING THE GROUP (20 minutes)
As each person arrives, greet him warmly. Update e-mail addresses and phone numbers.

When everyone has arrived, give each person several Post-It® notes and ask each one to write a thought about caring on each note. They can write a definition or words and phrases that come to mind when they think of the word "caring" or they can write their thoughts about what it means to care. (Take part in this activity yourself.) Then let each person share what he or she has written as he places his Post-It® note on the wall.

FOCUSING ON LIFE (10 minutes)
Ask: **Have you ever gotten lost?** (Briefly describe an experience of your own in which you were lost.) **How did you feel? Were you frightened? Did you feel that anyone knew or cared about your situation? Was there anything that gave you hope?** Ask the group to brainstorm words that express the feelings and situation of a person who is lost. Again, ask them to record their conclusions on Post-it® notes. Put those on the wall with the thoughts about caring. Let that serve as the backdrop for your meeting.

EXPLORING THE CHALLENGE (20 minutes)
Have a volunteer read Luke 19:10. The Scriptures describe a person who is without Christ as "lost." Review your group's descriptions of being lost (which you recorded under "Focusing on Life") and discuss which of them also apply to a person who is spiritually "lost." (Encourage your group members to begin to have "caring" compassion for people who are "lost" and do not know Jesus Christ.) Review your group's definitions of "caring" (which they wrote under "Building the Group").

Review the purpose of the Moving Toward Maturity series and the function of the Discipleship Group (page 132 of this Leader's Guide). State clearly the purpose of giving through *Giving Away Your Faith*. Stress the necessity of commitment to God and to one another in order for the Discipleship Group to be effective.

Distribute copies of the *Time Alone With God Notebook* (collect the money for both books). Encourage group members to continue their daily times alone with God during the Discipleship Group experience. Challenge them to discover God's desire for them to give away their faith as they read through the book of Acts.

Give everyone a copy of *Giving Away Your Faith*. Review the topics to be discussed, and read the group disciplines under "Personal Commitment" on page 11. Discuss any questions your students have about the commitments. State clearly that each person will move out of his comfort zone to boldly communicate the message of Jesus.

Briefly discuss the length and number of meetings (one hour per week with the group, plus individual study time, for the next ten weeks). Consult schedules and decide on a specific time and place to meet.

CONSIDERING THE CHOICE (10 minutes)
Ask who has fears about sharing Christ with friends who are not believers. Above all you do not want these very natural and typical fears to paralyze any student and prevent him from participating in this Discipleship Group. Assure your students that every Christian struggles with such fears about witnessing. Encourage each student to focus on his faith in Christ instead of on his fear. Let students catch your excitement about witnessing. Explain that you plan to go with each one when they meet with their non-believing friends over the next ten weeks.

Challenge the group to think and pray about making another 10-week commitment to the Discipleship Group. Anyone who decides not to become a part of this particular Discipleship Group should let you know before the next meeting and return the unmarked copies of *Giving Away Your Faith* and *Time Alone With God Notebook*.

Encourage everyone to set aside a specific time each week to complete the session to be discussed during the next Discipleship Group meeting.

Close by praying for each person by name. Thank God for your group and ask Him to give each one the compassion and the courage to share Christ with others.

Assignments for Next Week: Give the following assignments to those who decide to be a part of this Discipleship Group:
1. In *Giving Away Your Faith*, read pages 7-10 and study and sign the "Personal Commitment" (page 11).

2. Complete Session 1, and put together the Bible verse packet in the back of the book. (Show your group your packet to demonstrate what it looks like when it is put together. Remind group members to memorize John 17:3.)

3. Bring a Bible, a pen or pencil, and *Giving Away Your Faith* to every meeting.

Before students leave this first meeting, try to talk with them individually. See if they have questions or problems. Encourage them to commit themselves to the group, and let them know you care about each of them.

AFTER THE MEETING

1. Evaluate: Did each person become involved in the discussions? Are there people who need to be drawn out to participate more freely? Are there others who dominate? Review "Effective Meetings," pages 10-11 of this Leader's Guide.

2. This week, and every week, begin preparing for the next session at least five days in advance. Complete Session 1 in *Giving Away Your Faith*, and read through the Leader's Guide suggestions for your next meeting.

3. Schedule time to accompany students on their faith sharing assignments. It is crucial to the success of this group that students go with someone who knows how to communicate his faith. Your students will learn to witness by watching you share Christ.

If you are new at giving away your faith, go with a youth minister or pastor several times before leading young people through this experience. Then plan to make appointments with two students each week to meet with their non-believing friends. Place the group in pairs as they carry out their assignments with their non-believing friends. Team up those students with more experience sharing Christ with students with less experience.

S E S S I O N   1

Lost!

OVERVIEW

Key Concept   In order to communicate Jesus effectively, you must realize that people are lost without Jesus Christ.

Memory Verse   John 17:3

Goals   *Individual Growth:* To begin to have more compassion for people who do not know Christ.

                 Group Life: To agree to support one another in the new adventure of learning to share Christ.

BEFORE THE MEETING

1. Pray for each person who came to the last meeting, asking God to give each one the willingness to commit himself to the group and to share Christ.

2. In *Giving Away Your Faith*, do Session 1, writing your personal responses to each question. This week and every week, note in the margins other observations or personal experiences that relate to the lesson, and bring them up during your group meeting.

3. Memorize John 17:3.

4. Contact the group. Remind them of the meeting time and place, and answer any questions. If someone has decided not to participate in this Discipleship Group, assure the person that you still care for him and that you hope he will be able to participate in the future.

5. Make copies of e-mail addresses and phone numbers for each person.

6. Begin to think of people you know who do not know Jesus, and ask God to give you more compassion for them.

7. Gather materials for the meeting:
   • Bible
   • *Giving Away Your Faith*
   • Copies of group members' e-mail addresses and phone numbers

- Bible memory verses
- A picture of a very well-dressed person (from a magazine ad or clothes catalog)

THE MEETING

BUILDING THE GROUP (15 minutes)
Greet each person warmly as he arrives.

Confirm that by each person's presence, he is saying, "Yes, I want to be part of this Discipleship Group." Have everyone turn to the *Personal Commitment* sheet (page 11 in *Giving Away Your Faith*). Read it together. Have each person reaffirm his desire to follow through on these commitments. Ask anyone who hasn't signed the sheet to sign it now. (Be sure yours is signed!)

Ask volunteers to tell a little about the hardest part of keeping the commitments. Also ask how God helped them stay faithful to their Discipleship Group commitments, and how He picked them up when they did fall short. Add your own personal experience in keeping your commitments.

Assure your members that you are available to help them keep their commitments to this Discipleship Group. Have volunteers pray briefly for the Lord's help in maintaining the discipline and enthusiasm they will need, and for love and concern for each other and for non-Christians.

FOCUSING ON LIFE (15 minutes)
Show your students the picture of a very well-dressed person you have cut out of an ad. Give the person a name and summarize the following story:

This is _____. Just from looking at him [or her], what needs would you say _____ has? Would you say that money is one of his biggest needs? It doesn't look like it from the way he is dressed. But what if I were to tell you that I know _____ personally, and I happen to know that actually he is flat broke right now and he really does need money pretty badly. You see, _____ had a very good job — that's how he got those nice clothes. But he's just lost that job and has been looking for weeks for another one, but can't find anything. Nobody who meets him on the street would know that, because his sharp clothes are still left over from better days. But pretty soon they'll wear out, and if _____ doesn't find work, he won't be able to hide the fact that he is broke any longer.

Explain that this person's situation with money is something like many people's spiritual situation. They don't have Jesus Christ. Spiritually, they are empty, but their lives look pretty good on the outside. We tend to think they don't have any needs. Like fashionable clothes, their good appearances are only temporary and will wear out with time or with stress. The needs are there; it's just that most people cover them up so others don't see them.

EXPLORING GOD'S WORD (30 minutes)

(NOTE: Each week this section is based on the work students have done in *Giving Away Your Faith*. The discussion questions are usually not identical to those in the study book, but they draw from the same Scriptures and assignments. This helps students think through what they have studied rather than simply reading aloud their written answers.)

Allow time for group members to review their written responses for Session 1 in *Giving Away Your Faith*. Let them ask questions and make observations. Then discuss:

1. Do you think Romans 1:28-32 is a fair description of many people in our world today? (At first glance the passage appears to be talking about the grossest kinds of sinners. Yet it also lists the "little" sins such as envy, senselessness, faithlessness, disobedience to parents, etc.) **How should we look at people who do these kinds of things?**

2. Recall your description of a time when you were lost physically. (You did this last week.) **Now describe what you were like and how you felt when you were spiritually lost. How were you like the person described in Romans 1:28-32?**

3. When you think of your non-believing friends, do you have trouble seeing them in the condition described on pages 13-14? (characteristics of lost people) **Why is it hard to see some of our non-believing friends that way?** (They may seem to have everything together — maybe even better than we do!) Remember the diagram is God's viewpoint rather than our human viewpoint; He sees how people really are. Also, they may be like our friend _____ (the cutout from the ad) — looking just fine on the outside, but with desperate needs on the inside.

4. In this session you read about Jesus' attitude toward people who are lost. What would be some examples of showing that kind of attitude toward your non-believing friends? Be very specific.

Invite students to share their responses to "Loving Lost People" (pages

16-18 in *Giving Away Your Faith*). What characteristics does your student most need to work on? Help each one with these as you continue working through this Discipleship Group.

APPLYING GOD'S WORD (15 minutes)
Have students look over their answers to "Practical Hints On Loving Lost People" (pages 18-20 in *Giving Away Your Faith*). Ask them to choose one particular "hint" to work on this week. Let them know you are available to help them, and encourage them to help each other.

Have a time of prayer together. Ask the Lord to give you compassion for one particular lost friend, to see that person as Christ sees him and not as that person appears outwardly.

Assignments for Next Week: As you give the following assignments, express confidence that your students can and will carry them out and will succeed in their commitments to the Discipleship Group.

1. Have a time alone with God every day this week using the Bible readings at the end of Session 1.

2. Complete Session 2 in *Giving Away Your Faith*.

3. Memorize John 17:3. Review all of the memory verses you learned in *Following Jesus, Spending Time Alone with God*, and *Making Jesus Lord*.

4. Get together with a non-Christian friend and follow the instructions given in the lesson.

AFTER THE MEETING

1. Evaluate the meeting: How was the atmosphere? Relaxed? Too relaxed? Comfortable? If anything about the atmosphere did not seem right, jot it down, try to think of some reason for it, and try to determine what you can do to improve it for next week.

2. If any group member expressed special questions or problems, or was reluctant to sign the commitment sheet, either meet with that person this week or call him.

3. Begin to schedule time to meet with the non-believing friends of students in your group.

S E S S I O N 2

From Fear to Faith

OVERVIEW

Key Concept Natural fears about sharing Jesus Christ can be overcome through supernatural faith.

Memory Verses Romans 3:23; 6:23

Goals *Individual Growth:* To acknowledge and begin to overcome fears about witnessing.

Group Life: To accept each other's fears and encourage each other toward faith.

BEFORE THE MEETING

1. Pray for each group member, asking God to give each person honesty and courage.

2. In *Giving Away Your Faith*, do Session 2.

3. Think about your own fears about sharing Christ. Your present or past anxieties about witnessing will give you empathy for your students' fears.

4. Memorize Romans 3:23; 6:23.

5. Gather materials for the meeting:
   • Bible
   • *Giving Away Your Faith*
   • Bible memory verses

THE MEETING

BUILDING THE GROUP (15 minutes)

Warmly welcome each person. If you know of something specific that happened in someone's life this week (such as a sports event, an award, an illness in the family, a big test) mention it with appropriate congratulations, sympathy, concern, etc.

When everyone has arrived, begin by asking volunteers to share how the witness of particular people helped bring them to Christ. Be ready to share your own experience.

FOCUSING ON LIFE (10 minutes)

Discuss: **What are some typical childhood fears that you or others have had?** (Let students respond.) **What were some reasons for fearing those things?** (because they were unknown or unpredictable; because of a bad past experience, etc.) **How did you get over your childhood fear?** (learned more about it; someone else helped by setting an example; used will power to do it; etc.) Share an old fear of your own as you participate in the discussion. This discussion helps get students talking about their personal fears, but in a nonthreatening way, since they are bringing up past fears which may seem amusing now. For example, a little kid fears that he might go down the drain when the water was let out of the bathtub!

EXPLORING GOD'S WORD (30 minutes)

Have each student review Session 2 in *Giving Away Your Faith*. Ask for questions or observations about the session. Then discuss:

1. What might your old fears, those fears you've outgrown that we just talked about, have in common with the fear of sharing Christ with your friends? (The fear may be based on imagination or an inflated idea of how bad the outcome will be.)

2. Why are we ashamed to admit our fears? (want to appear strong and capable; don't want to admit weakness; scared we'll be laughed at; others depend on us and we don't want to let them down)

3. What's good about admitting fear? (gets it out in the open; gives other people the opportunity to help us; shows other people we're as human as they are; makes us more objective and rational about it; assures us we're normal; helps us depend on the Lord)

4. What are your biggest fears about sharing Christ with your friends? (Lead the way in admitting and talking about your fears of witnessing. As you share your own fears, you will help your students know that you understand. Encourage them to voice their fears.)

(NOTE: Individuals exist who have absolutely no fear of witnessing and do it all the time as a natural part of their lives. If you have someone like that in your group, you have several dynamics to deal with. The person who boldly witnesses may be impatient with those who are more reluctant to share Christ; he can't understand what's so frightening about it. The more hesitant person may feel inferior or less spiritual than the bolder witness. Yet more timid Christians can be spurred on by the enthusiasm of the one who is more bold. It is important for each person to respect one another's personalities and gifts and to help one another to communicate Christ more effectively.)

Discuss: **What do you have in common with the disciples in John 20:19-22? Which of the seven reasons for fear** (pages 26-29 in *Giving Away Your Faith*) **have you experienced? Which ones are you experiencing now?** (Encourage students to share openly.)

Ask: **What difference does it make to know that the resurrected Christ is with us?** (We can depend on Him for strength and guidance; we know He won't leave us.) **What practical steps can we take to help remind ourselves of the "sources of faith" on pages 29-32 of** *Giving Away Your Faith*? (Take time to consider concrete ways to be aware of Jesus' presence, peace, plan, penetration, and position.)

 APPLYING GOD'S WORD (10 minutes)
Have students turn to the prayer concerning fear (page 33 of *Giving Away Your Faith*).

Discuss particular fears about witnessing that students would like to pray about. Have a time of prayer about those fears. Then together, aloud have students pray for each other the prayer to overcome fear on page 33. (The place where individual students fill in the blank can be read silently by each person.)

Ask them to pair up and pray for each other during the next week.

Assignments for Next Week: As you give the following assignments, continue to express confidence in your students.

1. **Complete Session 3 in** *Giving Away Your Faith.*

2. **Continue having your daily time alone with God using the suggested Bible readings.**

3. **Memorize Hebrews 9:27.**

4. **Review memory verses from** *Following Jesus.* **These will help them share Christ more effectively.**

AFTER THE MEETING

1. Evaluate the meeting: Were students open about voicing their fears about witnessing? Were you honest with them about your own fears?

2. If any student seems to be withdrawing as the issue of witnessing gets more intense, call or spend some time with that person this week and express your confidence that he will grow in his faith by facing the fear.

3. If anyone is having problems keeping up a daily time alone with God, offer to phone the person in the middle of the week to ask how he is doing in his daily quiet times. Or meet with him to have a quiet time together.

S E S S I O N   3

Extraordinary Power

OVERVIEW

Key Concept   The Holy Spirit provides the power we need to witness for Christ.

Memory Verse   Hebrews 9:27

Goals   *Individual Growth:* To be filled continually with the Holy Spirit as you witness.

Group Life: To anticipate seeing the Holy Spirit use your group to bring people to Christ.

BEFORE THE MEETING

1. Pray for a fresh filling of the Spirit in your own life.

2. Pray for each person in the group to receive the Holy Spirit's power and experience that power daily.

3. In *Giving Away Your Faith*, complete Session 3.

4. Memorize Hebrews 9:27.

5. Gather materials for the meeting:
   - Bible
   - *Giving Away Your Faith*
   - An electrical appliance such as a hair dryer
   - Bible memory verses

THE MEETING

BUILDING THE GROUP (10 minutes)
After you have greeted the group, ask if anyone has noticed any changes in his fear concerning talking about Jesus. Ask for volunteers to talk about how they experienced fear and faith as they saw, prayed for, and/or talked to their non-believing friends. For some it will be a victory simply to have thought about the possibility of approaching someone

about Christ! Be positive about the group's honesty and encourage them to keep on looking for opportunities to communicate Christ.

FOCUSING ON LIFE (10 minutes)
Demonstrate your electrical appliance by plugging it in and using it. Then disconnect your appliance and ask the group why it won't work anymore. (It's cut off from its source of power. Without the power, it is useless. It does not do what it was made to do.)

Point out that the Holy Spirit is our source of power for witnessing (as well as for all other aspects of the Christian life). Cut off from Him, we can do nothing. With His power, we can be powerful and bold witnesses.

EXPLORING GOD'S WORD (35 minutes)
Have each student review Session 3 and ask questions or make comments. Then discuss:

1. What characteristics does a person have who tries to witness for Christ without relying on the power of the Holy Spirit? (argumentativeness, defensiveness, fear to the point of being silenced, attacking the person verbally, lack of love, resentment if the message doesn't get a response)

2. What difference will it make if we do rely on the Holy Spirit when we witness? (Our attitude and approach will be Christ-like; we'll witness with love, respect for the other person, good will, and faith that God will take care of the results.)

3. In which of the four areas of influence ("Jerusalem," "Judea," "Samaria," or the "ends of the earth," page 37-38 in *Giving Away Your Faith*) **do you find it easiest to witness? Why?** (Let students respond.) **In which area do you find it most difficult to witness, and why?** (Encourage group members to express their feelings as well as their thoughts.)

Ask students to describe the scene in Acts 2:1-4 when the disciples were filled with the Holy Spirit. Talk about times when you or your students have been particularly aware of the Holy Spirit's presence. Point out that He actively helps us even when we don't "feel" Him. We may not be aware of His help at the time.

Discuss the five signs of witnessing in the power of the Holy Spirit (pages 42-45 of *Giving Away Your Faith*) and ask the group to recount recent examples that they have seen or experienced with any of these five signs.

Ask: **When you witness, what results would you like to see? What results do you think you can expect immediately? Which ones might take longer? Which ones might you never see (although they will happen)?** (Let students respond.) **What's the connection between relying on the Holy Spirit and lives being changed because of our witnessing?** (Without the Spirit, we have no hope of lives being changed from our witness. Because we can count on lives changing even if they don't appear to be changed immediately.)

APPLYING GOD'S WORD (10 minutes)
Let students share questions they have about being filled with the Holy Spirit. Have a time of prayer for each student to be filled with the Spirit continually. The Holy Spirit has been offered as a gift; we need only to receive Him (Acts 19:1-7). Explain this to your group. Remind them that as they live filled with the Holy Spirit, they will have a desire and boldness to express Christ.

Assignments for Next Week: Notice that under "Making It Happen" your students are instructed to pray for and talk to a friend who doesn't know Christ. Give your students plenty of encouragement in this assignment, because some will be frightened. Invite students to phone you before or after their conversations and talk about how things went. Better yet, go with your students as they meet with their non-believing friends. Also give the following assignments:

1. Complete the Session 4 in *Giving Away Your Faith*.

2. Continue using the suggested Bible readings for your daily time alone with God.

3. Memorize Romans 5:8.

AFTER THE MEETING

1. Evaluate the meeting: Did students grasp the importance of being filled with the Spirit? Is it still vague or unclear to them? How did they react to the assignment to talk with a non-Christian friend?

2. If this first real witnessing opportunity seems to scare some of them ("I didn't know what I was getting into!") talk with that person privately and go with him to help him carry out the assignment.

A Friend in Need

OVERVIEW

Key Concept   We can make friends for Christ.

Memory Verse   Romans 5:8

Goals   *Individual Growth:* To begin making new friends and
             renewing old friendships with non-believers.

             Group Life: To look outside the confines of the group to
             see the needs of non-believers.

BEFORE THE MEETING

1. Pray for yourself and each person in the group to seek out new non-
   believing friends. Ask God to reveal to them people He wants each
   person to befriend.

2. Think of a non-believer to whom you can express friendship.

3. Complete Session 4 in *Giving Away Your Faith.*

4. Memorize Romans 5:8.

5. Gather materials for the meeting:
   - Bible
   - *Giving Away Your Faith*
   - Plastic fencing (from a toy barnyard set) or some similar
     material to make a miniature enclosure
   - Bible memory verses

THE MEETING

BUILDING THE GROUP (15 minutes)
After everyone has arrived (greeted warmly by you, of course) ask
for volunteers to share their experiences of trying to talk with
someone about Christ (part of this past week's assignments). Discuss how

the non-Christian friends were approached, how each person felt as they began conversations, how fears were handled, and what particular responses the friends made (both positive and negative). Express enthusiasm over good responses and offer encouragement to those whose friends tuned them out. You will not have time now to discuss problems and questions brought up by the non-Christian friends, but have them state those questions and problems, and offer to research them and talk them over next week.

FOCUSING ON LIFE (10 minutes)

Build your miniature "pen" and say something like: **Imagine this is a sheepfold, such as Jesus talked about in John 10. Jesus said that He Is the Good Shepherd and that we belong in His sheepfold because we belong to Him. But what would life be like for the sheep if they spent their entire lives inside the confines of that little sheepfold?** (Discuss how crowded, dirty, stinky, unhealthy, and boring that would be.) Summarize: **Jesus said He would lead us out so we can find pasture. Although it's safe inside the sheepfold, the adventure is outside of it. Making friends with and communicating Christ to non-believers is one of those blessings and advantages that can happen only outside the confines of our group of Christians.**

EXPLORING GOD'S WORD (30 minutes)

Let each student review Session 4 and make comments or ask questions.

Point out that many other things could be considered the main ingredients of friendship (having common interests, sharing similar goals, having similar life experiences); however, a friendship that has no compassion is not a true friendship and will not last when things get tough.

Discuss: **Describe a time when a person showed compassion to you.** (Let volunteers respond.) **How did you react? How did you feel about the person who was compassionate to you?** (response)

Summarize: **As we read the definition of Christian love in 1 Corinthians 13, its easy to see how far we fall short of that kind of love. Read through the chapter again, substituting the word "Jesus" for "love." Reading 1 Corinthians 13 in this way brings** home the fact that only Christ can love in such an ideal way. Because He lives in us by His Spirit (as you discovered last week) we can express His love to others.

Ask the group members to describe how friends have been comforters, counselors, and challengers to them. Discuss how each person can be a comforter, a counselor, and a challenger to a non-Christian friend.

As a group, read Philippians 2:3-4. Ask: **how can you show the attitude of Christ in your friendships with non-Christians?** (Let students respond.)

NOTE: As the leader, you should be aware that discussing friendships with non-believers raises some serious issues that probably your students will ask you about. They will ask you questions about going to bars and dating non-believers.

• Some students make friends very easily and naturally they already have built many bridges with non-Christians based on shared interests and activities. Those naturally winning ways need to be coupled with sincere concern for the spiritual welfare of their non-Christian friends. Otherwise they are merely popular and likable but not influencing their friends' lives. They may have their Christian and non-Christian relationships segregated so that they live in two different worlds. Many students don't carry their Christian lives over into their non-Christian friendships.

• On the other hand, there are students for whom friendship spells hurt and rejection. You may have students who make friends very slowly and hesitantly. It may be that their only friends are others in the Discipleship Group. Encourage the group to love and support each other, helping each person find the courage to make new friends with non-believers.

• Be sensitive to any parental misgivings about non-Christian friends. Many Christian parents do not want their teens to develop close relationships with non-Christians for fear of wrong influences. Certainly a Christian should be wary of developing a close relationship with a non-believer of the opposite sex, in the hope of winning that person to Christ. Talk with any parents who raise objections and explain the purpose of teaching students to reach out. Reassure parents with the fact that each of your students has the strong support of you and the entire Discipleship Group.

But ultimately the wishes of parents must be respected.

APPLYING GOD'S WORD (15 minutes)
Begin befriending non-Christians by spending time in prayer for them. Challenge each student in the group to pray for three particular people they know, or have the potential to know better, and sincerely desire that they know Jesus. This is not a gossip time, and names of people prayed for are not to go outside this group. While some non-Christians would appreciate being prayed for, others would be offended to find out people are praying for them (as though there's something wrong with them). You can use the guidelines for prayer under "Making It Personal" (pages 59-60 in *Giving Away Your Faith*).

Assignments for Next Week: As you make the following assignments, again express confidence in your students. Applaud them for making it this far in the Discipleship Group, and challenge them to successfully complete it.

1. **Complete Session 5 in** *Giving Away Your Faith.*

2. **Continue the daily Bible readings.**

3. **Memorize 1 Corinthians 15:3-4.**

4. **Review all memory verses from** *Following Jesus, Spending Time Alone with God,* **and** *Making Jesus Lord.*

AFTER THE MEETING

1. Evaluate the meeting: Do students seem eager to reach out to non-Christian friends? Are they reluctant? Dubious? Scared, but willing to try?

2. Does your own life reflect your willingness to make friends with non-believers?

S E S S I O N 5

Relate and Communicate

OVERVIEW

Key Concept   Turning a conversation toward the subject of Jesus
                     Christ opens the door for us to communicate the
                     Gospel.

Memory Verses   I Corinthians 15:3-4

Goals   *Individual Growth:* To learn how to turn a conversation
                     toward Jesus Christ.

                     Group Life: To practice conversing about Christ.

BEFORE THE MEETING

1. Pray for each of your students, for the friends to whom they want to
   witness, and for your own witness.

2. Recall conversations you have had about Jesus Christ – either someone
   else's witness to you, or your witness to someone else. Think of crucial
   points in the conversations and what made them crucial.

3. In *Giving Away Your Faith*, complete Session 5.

4. Memorize I Corinthians 15:3-4.

5. Gather materials for the meeting:
   • Bible
   • *Giving Away Your Faith*
   • Pencils and paper
   • Bible memory verses

THE MEETING

BUILDING THE GROUP (10 minutes)
If you made a new non-Christian friend this week, share the
experience. Ask the group to describe their own experiences. The Holy
Spirit may have opened some students' eyes to potential friends who need
Christ - people they had previously overlooked. Offer encouragement if
students are hanging back or unsure how to build friendship bridges. Say:

Tonight we're going to consider and practice some simple and practical ways of bringing Jesus Christ into a conversation.

FOCUSING ON LIFE (10 minutes)
Ask: **What was one conversation you had today that wasn't about Jesus Christ? How did you get into the conversation? How did you keep it going? How did the conversation end? Do you think you'll talk with that person about that subject again?** (As students respond to each question, discuss how their answers might apply to a conversation about Christ.)

EXPLORING GOD'S WORD (20 minutes)
Have students look over their responses to Session 5. Give them the opportunity to ask questions or make comments. Then discuss:

1. How did the woman at the well become aware that Jesus cared about her? (Jesus overcame cultural barriers to speak with her even though she was a Samaritan.)

2. What attitudes did He display toward her? (He was compassionate and loving, as well as concerned about her.)

3. What risks did He take in talking with her? (He was condemned for associating with a person considered "beneath" Him.)

4. What points in the conversation were crucial and how did He handle them? (Crucial points came up in John 4:9, 11, 17, 20, and 25 as Jesus fielded her questions and challenges.)

5. How did the woman try to distract Jesus from the real issue? (She asked questions that pointed out their differences and commented on side issues to change the subject.)

6. How did Jesus get back to the real issue? (He kept returning to her need to know Him.)

(NOTE: Point out to students that the Apostle John probably did not give us the entire conversation verbatim; what is written in John 4 may be the high points of a much longer talk.)

Distribute pencils and paper. Ask each group member to think of a friend that he has been particularly praying for and talking with – someone he sincerely wants to see know Jesus. Say: **Imagine yourself with your non-Christian friend at a time and place that you usually have an opportunity to talk. Write down all the questions and** statements you can think of that could turn a conversation toward Christ. After students have had time to brainstorm their conversation-starters, ask for volunteers to share what they have written.

APPLYING GOD'S WORD (20 minutes)
Divide the group into pairs. (If there is an odd number of students, pair one with you.) Have them practice an imaginary conversation about Christ – one person will be the "Christian" and the other the "non-Christian." (To get this started, you may want to demonstrate a conversation with a volunteer.) They should use principles discovered in Session 5 and in this session's discussion. It may help if the "non-Christian" plays the role of a particular person to whom the Christian actually desires to witness. You move around the room and tune in to the different conversations as unobtrusively as possible. When time is almost half gone, have the two people switch roles.

After you call time, ask whether anyone has questions or comments about his or her "practice" witnessing session. For some, playing the role may have been more nerve-wracking than actually communicating to a non-Christian! Discuss questions that came up and ask people if they felt they were either too "theological" or too vague in their answers.

Remind the group that this week begins the weekly assignment to share the Gospel with a non-Christian. Pray briefly for the people to whom people in the group want to witness, and for wisdom to know what to say and how to say it.

Assignments for Next Week: Give the following assignments:
1. Complete **Bible study 6** in *Giving Away Your Faith*.

2. Memorize 1 Peter 3:18.

3. Continue to spend time alone with God daily.

4. Memorize the four "Bridge Builders" questions and use them to carry on a conversation with a non-Christian friend.

AFTER THE MEETING

1. Evaluate the meeting: Was the role-play helpful? Are students coming up with practical and realistic ways to turn a conversation to the subject of Jesus Christ, or is their approach too theoretical, abstract, or phony?

2. Are you meeting your goals of going with your students to communicate Christ?

My Great Discovery

OVERVIEW

Key Concept   Preparation and practice makes perfect in presenting
our testimony.

Memory Verse   I Peter 3:18

Goals   *Individual Growth:* To write out a clear and concise testimony and present it to the group.

Group Life: To hear and give helpful comments about
each other's testimonies.

BEFORE THE MEETING

1. Pray for each person in your group. At this halfway point in the
Discipleship Group, ask God to encourage each one and give each one
renewed enthusiasm.

2. Complete Session 6 in *Giving Away Your Faith.*

3. Write out your own testimony according to the guidelines in Session 6.

4. Memorize I Peter 3:18.

5. Gather materials for the meeting:
   • Bible
   • *Giving Away Your Faith*
   • Pencils and paper
   • Bible memory verses

THE MEETING

BUILDING THE GROUP (10 minutes)
Take this opportunity to give your Discipleship Group several minutes of appreciation, affirmation, and a pep talk. Remind them that
they are now halfway through the sessions. Let them know that you are
proud of them for sticking with it – not just enduring it, but actively participating and keeping their commitments to the Lord and to each other.
Assure them that you know how tough the challenge of witnessing can

be. Once again remind them that you are available to help answer questions, offer an encouraging word, or go with them. (By this time you should have gone to meet a non-believer with each student at least once.) Mention that you pray regularly for each person in the group. Knowing that you care makes a world of difference to them!

 FOCUSING ON LIFE (10 minutes)
Pair off and tell each other about something positive that happened this week. (You pair up with someone if you have an odd number of students.) After students have shared with each other, get their attention again and say something like: **Wasn't that easy? It isn't hard to talk naturally about something positive that we've experienced. Believe it or not, talking about Christ can come just that easily and naturally. However, for reasons we've talked about in our earlier meetings, sometimes we get nervous when the conversation turns to Jesus. That's why it's helpful to know what we're going to say.** Emphasize that you're not talking about a pre-recorded announcement or a memorized speech, but intelligent preparation for making the case for Jesus Christ.

NOTE: Some Christians think it is unspiritual to have a set plan, either written out or in our heads, for what we are going to say when we witness. They believe — and rightly so — that the Holy Spirit will lead us as we speak. Although Jesus told us not to *worry* about what we are to say (Matthew 10:19), He did not tell us not to *think* about it. We can best speak for the Lord when we are prepared. Unprepared, we ramble or include irrelevant experiences which confuse the listener or detract from the main point.

EXPLORING GOD'S WORD (20 minutes)
Give students the opportunity to look over their responses to Session 6, make comments, and ask questions.

Read Paul's testimony before King Agrippa in Acts 26:1-23. Discuss: **How would you describe Paul's attitude and approach as he gave his testimony?** (Note Paul's respect for his listener; his confidence in his experience with Christ; his brief but honest description of his former life before meeting Jesus; his convincing, detailed story of his personal encounter with Jesus; and his care in giving God the credit.) You may also want to read verses 24-29 and note the confidence and presence of mind with which Paul rose above Festus' insults and Agrippa's resistance, with calmness and humor.

Hand out pencils and paper and give students the assignment of writing out their testimonies according to the guidelines on pages 73-75 of *Giving Away Your Faith*. Use the three-point outline given, and consider the questions listed. (Be available to answer students' questions and provide help. You should have written your own testimony already.)

APPLYING GOD'S WORD (20 minutes)

Ask for volunteers to present their testimonies to the rest of the group. Present your own testimony after several students have read theirs.

Invite the group to give *helpful* and *positive* encouragement after each person's testimony. Then, before going on to the next one, have them write down two improvements that could make the testimony better. Follow the guidelines in the book. If something in a person's testimony doesn't communicate and doesn't make sense, it's better for him to discuss that with his supportive Discipleship Group than with the non-believer he's trying to convince. Yet there are kind and unkind ways to express to a person that he's not communicating. Be positive.

The purpose of writing and giving a critique of the testimonies is to help students continue to polish their testimonies and give them an increasing sense of being well prepared to talk about Jesus Christ. Once all testimonies have been read and spoken, and written feedback given, ask them to rewrite their testimonies during the week. Assure them that you are available to read or listen to their revised efforts.

Assignments for Next Week: Instruct students to continue working on their written testimonies. Give the following assignments:

1. Complete Session 7 in *Giving Away Your Faith*.

2. Memorize Mark 11:15 and continue the daily Bible reading in Acts.

3. Rewrite, condense, and memorize your testimony.

AFTER THE MEETING

1. Evaluate the meeting: Did students' testimonies sound natural and convincing?

2. Is there someone who needs special encouragement with his testimony? Make a point of calling or meeting with that person this week.

SESSION 7

The Message

OVERVIEW

Key Concept   We can present the message of Christ clearly.

Memory Verse   Mark 1:15

Goals   *Individual Growth:* To become comfortable presenting the Gospel.

                 Group Life: To encourage each other in sharpening our skills in presenting the Gospel.

BEFORE THE MEETING

1. Pray for your group. Ask God to give them freedom and confidence in presenting the Gospel.

2. Pray for yourself, that you will continue to be a positive, enthusiastic example in sharing Christ.

3. Complete Session 7 in *Giving Away Your Faith*, including becoming familiar with the "Jesus: No Equal" booklet.

4. Memorize Mark 1:15.

5. Gather materials for the meeting
   • Bible
   • *Giving Away Your Faith*
   • Sets of instructions (such as a recipe, a diagram for assembling a model airplane, rules of a game, etc.)
   • Bible memory verses

THE MEETING

BUILDING THE GROUP (10 minutes)
As group members arrive, greet each one warmly. Let them know that this Discipleship Group is more than a habit or an obligation, it's

an important time to encourage each other in our faith.

Get the group into pairs to read their revised written testimonies to each other. Have one group as a whole offer two ways that the person making the presentation can improve that presentation.

Say: **We're doing a good job with learning how to present a clear, brief, and convincing testimony about what Christ has done for us. But when our friends ask heavier questions about what it all means, who Christ really is, or how the Christian life works, we need to be ready.** Emphasize the need for solid facts about God and about salvation. Explain that our faith is more than our personal experience; it's the truth.

FOCUSING ON LIFE (5 minutes)

Show your students the various instructions you have brought to the meeting. Ask: **Why do we need written instructions for how to do things?** (so we're not left guessing; so we don't waste time making mistakes; so the results will be what they're supposed to be; because the writer of the instructions has better understanding than we do) Ask for some other examples of things that need written instructions.

Say: **We appreciate and use a good, clear set of instructions for almost everything. Presenting Christ to someone is no different. We can use a clearly written explanation of the facts to help explain the Gospel to our friends.**

EXPLORING GOD'S WORD (30 minutes)

Discuss students' responses to the Session questions as you go through the "Jesus: No Equal" booklet together. Touch on each "reality" even if you do not have time to answer every study question. As you go through the material together, ask students to bring up any questions they think their non-Christian friends might have about any of the points in the booklet. Write those questions as you go, then assign the questions to volunteers to research and come back with a thorough answer.

APPLYING GOD'S WORD (20 minutes)

Have students pair off (as usual, you will be with one student if you have an odd number). One person of each pair will be the believer reading the "Jesus: No Equal" booklet; the other person will play the role of a non-Christian friend who has expressed interest in knowing about Christ. Have students practice presenting the "Jesus: No Equal" booklet to one another.

Discuss any snags students ran into during their role-playing.

Assignments for Next Week:
1. Complete Session 8 in *Giving Away Your Faith*.

2. Memorize John 1:12 and continue daily Bible readings in Acts.

3. Continue to review the memory verses from previous books.

AFTER THE MEETING

1. Evaluate the meeting: Were students comfortable using the "Jesus: No Equal" booklet? Did any students have particular problems using it?

2. As they practice their testimonies and the Gospel presentation, is the group's attitude and approach toward communicating Christ staying fresh and spontaneous, or are they falling into a rut of reciting learned material? The key to keeping them "on the edge" is having them put this into practice every week. As the leader, you can continue to set the example of a person who is enthusiastic and natural about sharing Christ.

3. Are you going out with students to share their faith each week?

S E S S I O N   8

Drawing the Net

OVERVIEW

Key Concept	Focus on the importance of bringing our non-believing friends to the point of making a definite decision about Jesus Christ.
Memory Verse	John 1:12
Goals	*Individual Growth:* To develop confidence and sensitivity about helping someone make a decision to follow Christ.
	Group Life: To express confidence in each other's ability to lead someone to Christ.

BEFORE THE MEETING

1. Pray for each person in your Discipleship Group and for their non-Christian friends by name.

2. Based on your most recent experience of "drawing the net" (leading someone to accept Christ) think about how you reached that point in the conversation, how you led the person to a decision, and how the person responded.

3. Complete Session 8 in *Giving Away Your Faith.*

4. Memorize John 1:12.

5. Gather materials for the meeting:
   - Bible
   - *Giving Away Your Faith*
   - Bible memory verses

THE MEETING

BUILDING THE GROUP (10 minutes)
After everyone has arrived, ask who they tried to communicate Christ to this week. Find out what happened, what the response was,

and what questions were brought up. If a non-Christian friend has accepted Christ, have a time of prayer and thanksgiving, asking God to strengthen and teach that new behavior. If some of their friends are close to following Jesus, intercede for them.

 FOCUSING ON LIFE (10 minutes)
Ask: **What's one thing you have learned to do in the past year? How did you learn to do it? Who taught you?** (Discuss answers.) **Could you have learned without someone to teach you?**

Point out that people want to find Jesus Christ, but most don't know how. They need someone to help them. Even after they know all the facts about Jesus, they need to make a personal decision to accept Him. Emphasize that if we simply give people the facts and don't give them the opportunity to accept Christ, we've left them hanging without knowing what to do. We need to learn to "draw the net" and bring that person to Christ.

 EXPLORING GOD'S WORD (30 minutes)
Have a volunteer read Acts 8:26-40. This is an excellent biblical example of a faithful witness, Philip, explaining the Gospel clearly and then effectively drawing the net.

Ask: **Why might Philip have been surprised that the Holy Spirit led him toward Gaza?** (He may not have expected to find any potential converts to Christ in Gaza. The road was a desert road. He was already reaching thousands.) **What are some unexpected ways that we, or people we know, have come to know Christ?** (Discuss answers.) **What does that tell us?** (Everyone we talk to is a potential follower of Jesus.)

How did Philip know the Ethiopian might be interested in Jesus? (He was reading the Scriptures. God spoke to him.) **What are some signals our friends send us that indicate they might be interested in Jesus?** (They ask questions or talk about spiritual matters.)

The Ethiopian showed unusual willingness to be led and instructed. Discuss what we can do when a person shows some interest in Christ, yet also puts up some resistance or responds with apathy. (listen patiently; pray; keep a loving attitude; etc.)

Think of some ways the Ethiopian could have side-tracked Philip. Why did that not happen? (Philip kept the Scripture passage and Jesus as the center of the conversation.)

(NOTE: Verse 37, Philip's "net-drawing" statement, does not appear in all ancient biblical manuscripts and so is relegated to a footnote in modern translations. However, believing in Jesus as the Son of God is crucial in biblical accounts of conversion, such as in Peter's first sermons in Acts 2-4, Paul's conversion in Acts 9:20, and Romans 10:9. We can be sure that Philip would never have baptized the Ethiopian unless he were sure that the man truly believed in Jesus.)

Ask: **Did anyone act as a "Philip" for you to help lead you to Christ? Who? How did it happen? Would you like to be a "Philip" for friends who need Christ?** Point out that any follower of Jesus can have that privilege if he or she is willing to draw the net and bring a non-Christian friend to a point of decision.

APPLYING GOD'S WORD (10 minutes)
Spend this time praying for your non-Christian friends and for yourselves. Ask God to give you the wisdom, courage, determination, and sense of timing to bring your friends to a point of deciding about Jesus. Pray for each non-believing friend. Pray that their minds and hearts will open up and that they will meet Jesus. Ask God for sensitivity to friends' moods, feelings, and readiness to be serious about following Christ.

Assignments for Next Week: Assure your students of your prayers and support before you make the following assignments:

1. Complete Session 9 in *Giving Away Your Faith*.

2. Memorize Revelation 3:20 and continue daily readings in Acts.

3. Review Session 8 and memorize the key questions to ask a non-Christian friend. Be prepared to answer objections he might present.

AFTER THE MEETING

1. Evaluate the meeting: Do students have confidence that they can draw the net and help someone accept Christ, or are they hesitant and nervous?

2. Are you keeping up with your own time alone with God and regular prayer for yourself and your students?

3. Are you meeting with your students each week as they meet with their non-believing friends?

SESSION 9

Hard Questions

OVERVIEW

Key Concept Difficult questions about Jesus Christ do not have to intimidate us, because there are excellent answers.

Memory Verse Revelation 3:20

Goals *Individual Growth:* To have confidence that tough questions about Jesus Christ can be answered.

Group Life: To assist each other in handling tough questions by sharing answers.

BEFORE THE MEETING

1. Pray for God's insight into difficult questions and for His insight into the hearts of people who ask them.

2. Complete Session 9 in *Giving Away Your Faith.*

3. If one of the questions in the session (or another question) particularly bothered you before you were a Christian, consider how God either answered it or caused it to become less important to you.

4. Memorize Revelation 3:20.

5. Gather materials for the meeting:
   - Bible
   - *Giving Away Your Faith*
   - Bible memory verses

THE MEETING

BUILDING THE GROUP (10 minutes)
Since this is your next-to-last meeting before finishing this book, express your appreciation to the group for their faithfulness and growth. Tell them that next week's meeting will begin with a special time

of praise to God for what He has done during these weeks.

FOCUSING ON LIFE (10 minutes)
Pick out a student who is particularly accomplished at a musical instrument, a sport, or some other acquired skill. Ask the student to describe some of the biggest challenges in becoming skillful at what he does. Ask: **When you came up against a "wall" – some technique that seemed too difficult, some level of accomplishment that you didn't think you could reach – what did you do?** (The student had to keep working at finding a solution, or else give up. The student's level of accomplishment proves that he or she did not give up, but persevered, seeing the difficulty as a challenge rather than as an obstacle. Of course, there was probably a persistently encouraging coach, teacher, or parent in the background too.)

Summarize: **Sometimes our non-Christian friends will raise very difficult questions about Jesus Christ. We can fold up in the face of those questions, or we can take them on as challenges and find answers. We never need to fear investigating the reality and truth about Jesus Christ. Jesus said that He is the truth (John 14:6) and therefore no truth that we discover can ever contradict Him.**

EXPLORING GOD'S WORD (25 minutes)
Discuss your students' responses to the Bible study of Acts 17 (pages 103-104 of *Giving Away Your Faith*). Point out how Paul "reasoned with them from the Scriptures" (v. 2) and how he concentrated on the historical person of Jesus Christ (v. 3). Paul kept his purpose clear and founded his arguments firmly on the Word of God. Notice also that even Paul did not convince everyone, for only "some of the Jews were persuaded" (v. 4).

Ask: **What is the difference between "Epicurean" and "Stoic" philosophers?** (v. 18) (They were from two opposite schools of thought. The Epicureans believed in eating, drinking, and being merry, enjoying life's pleasures to the fullest. The Stoics had a stark, dark, disengaged view of life.) Point out that while we may have friends of both types, both can be attracted to Jesus Christ.

Explain that Paul took advantage of the Athenians' natural curiosity about new ideas (vv. 20-21) to introduce the Good News of Jesus. He commended them for what they were doing right (worshiping, v. 23, although they did not know the true God).

Ask: **What were the three different responses to Paul's message in verses 32-34?** (Some people sneered; some were interested; some became believers.) Explain that they will see all three responses as they continue to present Christ faithfully. Take comfort in knowing that even Paul encountered all three responses to his preaching.

Ask which of the "Tough Questions" dealt with in this Bible study (pages 105-115) have come up in your students' witnessing. How did your students answer them? Which questions do students fear most? For which questions was this session particularly helpful? Ask students to raise other questions which their non-Christians friends have brought up.

Try to narrow down the "Tough Questions" to one or two which concern your group the most.

APPLYING GOD'S WORD (20 minutes)
Take the particularly tough question (or questions) which you and your group have selected, and spend this time talking it over, using Session 9, your own study, and your own experience to arrive at useful answers. Urge all group members to participate even if they think their comments are not very profound. Remind them that we never know what answer the Holy Spirit will use to strike a convincing note with our friends. Have students pair off to discuss the rest of the tough questions in Session 9.

Even as you discuss how to answer the objections of non-Christians, it is important to remember that some people ask tough questions because they sincerely want answers; others ask tough questions as a distraction. But in either case, when every question has been laid to rest, the person still must make a personal decision about what he or she will do with Jesus Christ.

Pray together for wisdom to understand God's truth and to understand the hearts of your non-believing friends.

Assignments for Next Week: As you give students their final assignments in this book, be positive about their progress, and let them know you look forward to a very special meeting next week.

1. Complete Session 10 in *Giving Away Your Faith*.

2. Memorize 2 Corinthians 5:17, and continue daily readings in Acts.

3. Continue to review the memory verses from the other books.

4. Share your testimony and the "Jesus: No Equal" booklet with at least one friend this week.

AFTER THE MEETING

1. Evaluate the meeting: Did students grasp the fact that tough questions don't have to intimidate them, but instead can challenge them to grow and know Christ better?

2. Are any students discouraged because they haven't led anyone to Christ during these weeks and feel like they have "failed" this course? Assure them that God wants them to be faithful witnesses, then He will take care of who comes to know Him.

3. Have you fulfilled your goal of taking students to meet with their non-Christian friends?

S E S S I O N   1 0

Getting Started

OVERVIEW

Key Concept   New believers need tender loving care and focused attention from you in order to grow in their relationship to Christ.

Memory Verse   2 Corinthians 5:17

Goals   *Individual Growth:* To take the challenge to help a new Christian grow.

Group Life: To praise God together for what He has done for you in this Discipleship Group.

BEFORE THE MEETING

1. Pray for each group member. Thank God for giving you the opportunity to know each one. Continue to pray for their witness and their non-believing friends.

2. Complete Session 10 in *Giving Away Your Faith*.

3. Memorize 2 Corinthians 5:17.

4. Write out the positive things that have happened in your life and your students' lives as a result of this Discipleship Group. Write out constructive criticisms also.

5. Familiarize yourself with *Getting Started*, the follow-up booklet.

6. Gather materials for the meeting:
   - Bible
   - *Giving Away Your Faith*
   - *Getting Started*
   - Set of baby clothes
   - Bible memory verses

THE MEETING

BUILDING THE GROUP (15 minutes)
Welcome each person warmly. Say specific words of appreciation for each person.

As you promised last week, this meeting will begin with a time of praise to the Lord for what He has done for you during this Discipleship Group. Ask students to share particular Scriptures that have been meaningful to them during these weeks. Pray together, thanking God for giving you a heart for reaching your non-believing friends and for equipping you to share Christ with them in confidence.

Invite the group to express several special things this study has meant to them. (You participate along with them.)

FOCUSING ON LIFE (5 minutes)

Show students the set of baby clothes and ask them if they can remember ever wearing clothes of such a tiny size. Of course, none of us can remember that far back, yet we were all babies who wore that size clothes and who needed constant care and attention. Point out that "baby" Christians are like that. Down the road they will be able to stand on their own, but for now they need an extra amount of care.

EXPLORING GOD'S WORD (30 minutes)

Have students look over their written responses to Session 10 and ask questions or make comments.

Ask: **What are some practical ways you can give focused attention to a new Christian this week?** (Discuss answers.)

What are some ways you can protect a new believer this week? (Of course you cannot follow a new Christian around and protect him from every bad situation. But you can look out for him. Notice if he is coming under bad influences, is getting discouraged, or is facing temptation. You can step in and offer comfort and help, offering that person encouragement. And you can pray for his protection from Satan.)

Discuss: **How do you feel about taking responsibility for helping a new Christian grow?** (eager to help; obligated; inconvenienced; glad to be needed, etc.) Explain that Jesus asks us to inconvenience ourselves for the sake of others, looking "not only to your own interests, but also to the interests of others" (Phil. 2:4). When we lead someone to Christ, or when God brings a baby Christian across our path, we have a responsibility to help that person. It is a commitment we can make to Christ for the sake of that new believer. Who is the new believer you want to meet with?

Go through *Getting Started* and discuss how to use it most effectively to help a new, young Christian grow. Students will take on the leadership role which you - the leader of this Discipleship Group - have fulfilled and modeled for them these past months. Using the section "Meeting Together" as a guide, students will meet with a new believer for six weeks. Stress that students should have a caring and loving approach as they offer help to new Christians. They are not simply meeting to "go through a booklet" with someone, but to maintain a warm, personal contact with someone who needs them.

 APPLYING GOD'S WORD (20 minutes)
Pray for the new Christians the students have chosen to meet with and for your students who will help them grow.

Close the meeting with another time of singing and prayers of thanksgiving.

You may also use this time to encourage students to participate in the next Discipleship Group, using Book 5 in the Moving Toward Maturity series, *Influencing Your World.*

Try to talk with each person before he leaves the meeting. Thank each one for the faithfulness shown to the group and to the Lord. Express your confidence that your students will go on sharing Christ in the power and love of the Holy Spirit.

Assignments: Encourage group members to carry out these continuing assignments.
1. Continue to share your testimony and the "Jesus: No Equal" booklet every week.

2. Continue to meet with your new Christian friends, helping them grow in their relationship with Jesus Christ.

3. Continue having your time alone with God.

AFTER THE MEETING

1. Continue taking students to talk to non-believing friends.

2. Contact each person in the group a week or so before the next Discipleship Group starts. Encourage each person to continue a commitment to the group.

NOTES

INFLUENCING YOUR WORLD

Leader's Guide prepared by
Barry St. Clair and Sandy Larsen

Leading Your Discipleship Group

Moving Toward Maturity is a five-part discipleship training series for young people. It is designed to help them become independently dependent on Jesus Christ and then teach others to do the same. This series has four main purposes:

1. To encourage students to passionately pursue Jesus Christ.
2. To help young people develop strong, Christ-like character.
3. To train young people in the "how to's" of Christian living.
4. To move young people from the point of getting to know Jesus Christ to the point of offering Him to others.

Influencing Your World, the final book in the series, challenges students to reach out to others through their own ministries and to disciple others. Your group will discover compassion, spiritual gifts, and serving others. They will learn to meet people's needs and multiply their lives through leading their own discipleship group. The other four study books in the series and related materials are described on the outside back cover of this Leader's Guide.

IMPORTANT NOTE: This Leader's Guide contains vital instructions, hints, and direction to help you lead your group most effectively. **We have placed this important information in only one place in the Leader's Guide, pages 7-11 in the *Following Jesus* section of the Leader's Guide.** Each time you begin a new book, review thoroughly the "Leading Your Discipleship Group" material. By doing so, you will sharpen your own leadership abilities. Through God's Spirit and your investment, students' lives will change.

SCRIPTURE MEMORY NOTE: Each Moving Toward Maturity book contains Bible memory verses that students memorize each week. These verses are found on the last page of each book. Since students tend to have trouble memorizing verses, your encouragement will help them succeed. The design of these books does not allow us to provide removable Scripture memory cards. Help by giving them ten small blank cards with a rubber band. Each week, when you make the assignments, have them write out the verse for the week on the card. Encourage them to carry the verses with them to review during the week. Keep extra cards in case they lose them. Helping your students succeed in memorizing Scripture is one of the greatest gifts you can give them!

INTRODUCTORY SESSION

Continuing Your Discipleship Group

OVERVIEW

Key Concept   To discover how to minister to other people so that each student uniquely influences his own world.

Goals   *Individual Growth:* To understand and experience what it means to have a ministry to other people through participating in the discipleship group.

Group Life: To practice ministry with each other and to encourage each other in ministry to friends at school.

BEFORE THE MEETING

1. Study pages 7-11 of this Leader's Guide for important background information.

2. In *Influencing Your World,* study pages 1-11, and put together the Bible memory packet found in the back of the book.

3. Phone each person who said that he or she would come to the first *Influencing Your World* Discipleship Group meeting. Your group should consist of people who have been through *Following Jesus, Spending Time Alone with God, Making Jesus Lord,* and *Giving Away Your Faith.* Ask everyone to bring their school and work schedules with them to the first meeting.

4. Be prepared to review the purpose of the Moving Toward Maturity series for the group. See pages 7-11 of this Leader's Guide.

5. Pray for each person in the Discipleship Group. Ask God to give each one the confidence that he can have a ministry with other people.

6. Gather the materials for the meeting:
   - Bible
   - *Influencing Your World*
   - 3" x 5" cards
   - Pencils
   - Bible memory verses
   - Poster board on which you have fastened several objects (such as product labels, money, pens, picture, etc.)
   - List of questions about the objects on the poster board (see

Focusing on Life for explanation)
- Paper
- *Time Alone with God Notebook* for each person

THE MEETING

BUILDING THE GROUP (10 minutes)
As each person arrives, greet him warmly. Update addresses and e-mails. Inquire about special things going on (sports, drama, tests, college applications, driver's education, dating, etc.).

FOCUSING ON LIFE (15 minutes)
Tell the group you are going to give them an observation test. Hand out paper and pencils to everyone. Say: **I'm going to hold up something for you to look at. I'll give you 10 seconds to observe it. Then I'll give you one minute to write down everything you've seen, then I'm going to ask you a series of questions about what you have observed.**

Hold up the poster board with all the objects and count off 10 seconds.

Turn the poster board around and give students one minute to write down their observations.

Now ask questions to test students' observation skills. (For example: **What brand of lemonade was the label from? What color dress was the model wearing? Whose picture was on the bill? Was there a poem on the board?**)

Check the accuracy of the students' answers.

Say: **Some of you may be better observers than others. But one thing about observing is that we can always get better at it. The more you practice observing things, the more you notice. If I gave you the same sort of test next week, you would probably do even better than you did tonight.**

Ask students to write down the names of one to five people they saw today who had some kind of problem (mental, physical, financial). **How did you know of the problems?** (person looked depressed; person on crutches; car broken down) This will focus attention on observing people's needs.

Observing objects on a poster is just a fun exercise. But being able to observe life, to see what is happening with other people, to see their needs — that's something close to God's heart. In this Discipleship Group we will learn how to see people's needs

and how to minister to people in Jesus' name.

EXPLORING THE CHALLENGE (20 minutes)

Have group members turn their papers over and make two columns. On the left side ask them to write names of people they know personally who have needs, and on the right side, what those needs are. They will not share these lists out loud.

Say: **If you've been able to write down several names, or even one name, then you have already been observing your friends' lives and have picked up on their needs. But what can we do about those needs? We may not have all the answers, but in Christ we can have compassion and power to help other people. That's what we want to commit ourselves to do in this 10-week Discipleship Group.**

Review the purpose of the Moving Toward Maturity series. Invite students to share some things they have learned or experienced through previous Discipleship Groups. Stress the need for commitment to Christ and to one another in order for this final Discipleship Group to be effective. Ask them to stay intense and focused until you "cross the finish line."

Distribute copies of the *Time Alone with God Notebook*. Encourage group members to continue their daily times alone with God. Challenge them to grow in Christ on their own outside the group as they read through 1 and 2 Thessalonians, 1 and 2 Timothy, and Titus.

Give everyone a copy of *Influencing Your World*. (Remind them to pay you for both books.) Review the topics, and read the group disciplines (pages 8-10). Discuss any questions students may have.

Briefly describe the time required for this experience (one hour to one and a half hours per week with the group, individual study time, one and a half to two hours per week in the Group Ministry Project, and practical projects in ministry in the lunchroom at school). This Discipleship Group will probably demand more time than the others. Be up front about that. Encourage them by assuring them that they can handle more because of their growth and maturity.

Have them look at their schedules and decide what specific times and places to meet.

CONSIDERING THE CHOICE (10 minutes)

Challenge the group to think and pray about making another 10-week commitment to the Discipleship Group. Let them know that you are fully willing to commit the necessary time to the group, and while school and family responsibilities must come first, you are confident that they can find (or make) time in their schedules to carry out the study and projects. Offer to help them set goals and plan their schedules.

Anyone who decides not to become a part of this Discipleship Group needs to let you know before the next meeting and return his unmarked copies of *Influencing Your World* and *Time Alone with God Notebook*.

Encourage everyone to set aside a specific time each week to complete the session for the next Discipleship Group meeting.

Close by praying for each person, including yourself. Each person pray for the person on his right, thanking God for each other. Ask God to give each of you the sensitivity to see other people's needs and the willingness to try to meet those needs in Jesus' strength.

Assignments for Next Week:
1. In *Influencing Your World,* read pages 7-10, study and sign the "Personal Commitment" sheet (page 11).

2. Complete Session 1 and put together the memory verse packet found in the back of the book.

3. Memorize Matthew 9:36-38.

4. Bring a Bible, a pen or pencil, and *Influencing Your World* to every meeting.

Before students leave this first meeting, try to talk with each one. See if there are questions, problems, or misgivings about participating in the Discipleship Group. Encourage them to make the commitment, and let them know you are committed to each one of them.

AFTER THE MEETING

1. Evaluate: Did each person become involved in the discussions? Are some members too dominant, others too shy? Are group relationships still strong? Was everyone comfortable at the meeting? Review "Effective Meetings," pages 10-11 of this Leader's Guide.

2. This week, and every week, begin preparing for the next session at least five days in advance. Complete Session 1 in *Influencing Your World,* and read through the Leader's Guide suggestions for your next meeting.

Book Five − Influencing Your World

S E S S I O N 1

Broken Hearts

OVERVIEW

Key Concept   We can have compassion for people in the same way Jesus did.

Memory Verses   Matthew 9:36-38

Goals   *Individual Growth:* To begin to see the needs of others and become confident that in Christ we can help meet those needs.

Group Life: To be reassured that we are not alone as we minister to others.

BEFORE THE MEETING

1. Pray for each person in your Discipleship Group. Ask God to show you specific needs which you can help meet.

2. In *Influencing Your World,* complete Session 1, writing your personal answers to each question. This week and every week, note in the margins other observations or personal experiences that relate to the lesson, and bring them up during your group meeting.

3. Memorize Matthew 9:36-38.

4. Contact each person, remind him of the meeting time and place, and answer any questions. If someone decides not to participate in this Discipleship Group, assure that person that you still care for him.

5. Give each person a copy of the updated address information. Make enough copies for each group member to have one.

6. Gather materials for the meeting:
   • Bible
   • *Influencing Your World*
   • Copies of updated group information
   • Bible memory verses
   • pencils/pens
   • paper

THE MEETING

BUILDING THE GROUP (15 minutes)

Greet each person warmly as he arrives. Have everyone turn to the "Personal Commitment" sheet (page 11 in *Influencing Your World*) and read it together. Each person should have already signed the commitment sheet; ask anyone who hasn't to sign it now. (Be sure yours is signed!)

Ask volunteers to offer brief prayers for the Lord's help in keeping your commitments to the Discipleship Group.

FOCUSING ON LIFE (15 minutes)

Ask students to take paper and pencils and make a list of the five biggest needs facing students today. You may have students do this individually or in groups of two or three.

Ask volunteers to share their lists. Undoubtedly many students will have come up with identical needs while some will have mentioned needs others did not. Try to narrow down the lists to five common needs of students.

Discuss: **Is there any need on this list which Christ could not meet?** Some needs, such as purpose in life or forgiveness for sins, are obviously spiritual, and Jesus is obviously involved in the solution. Other needs, at first glance, don't appear so spiritual, such as finding a job after graduation. Discuss how a relationship with Christ makes a difference in those more "down-to-earth" needs also. For example, a person looking for a job can trust the Lord to guide him, to prepare him for interviews, and to provide for his needs even if he doesn't find the particular job he wants.

Jesus had compassion on people and met their needs, whether spiritual or physical. That's what Session 1, "Broken Hearts", is all about.

EXPLORING GOD'S WORD (30 minutes)

(NOTE: Each week this section is based on the work students have done in *Influencing Your World*. The discussion questions are not the same as those in the student's book, but they draw from the same Scriptures and assignments. This helps students think through what they have studied rather than simply repeating their written answers aloud.)

Discuss: **How did Jesus view the people in Matthew 9:36? How do each of the three descriptions Jesus used of people then ("harassed," "helpless," "like sheep without a shepherd") also describe people today?**

How did you feel when you read statistics about crime, abortion, abuse, drugs, suicide, etc., in this chapter? What can we do to make those overwhelming statistics more personal? (Think of particular individuals you know who have been victims or perpetrators of crime, have drug or alcohol problems, misuse sex, are in unhealthy families, and so forth. Put names with the statistics.)

Jesus saw the hurting crowd as sheep without a shepherd. Then He changed the metaphor (v. 37) and referred to a "harvest." In what sense are those people with such serious problems a potential harvest? (God can bring them in to His kingdom. They are out there waiting to be gathered. It takes work by willing laborers.)

Select one or two specific problems of friends of your students. Talk through how knowing Jesus can help those friends honestly face and deal with their problems. Stress that Jesus may not take all the problems away but He will be with that person and living in the person to work through the problem. If we don't see Jesus as the ultimate answer, we won't have much motivation to help our hurting friends find Him.

Discuss: **Why do so few students seem willing to be laborers for Christ in their schools?** (Fear of being laughed at; reluctance to be different from the crowd; too busy with other things; feel that no one else is doing it so why should they.)

Does it surprise you that Christ would want to use us as His laborers to help bring people to Him? Why doesn't He do it Himself? (He does do it — through us – though. Of course, He can speak directly to any student's heart. But He wants to involve us.)

How did you feel when you read "Making It Personal" (page 20-21) and discovered that you will become a laborer for Christ during your lunch period at school? (Scared? Afraid of being used by others? Confused about how to do it? Wishing you'd never gotten into this?) **Don't back out before you've given it a try!**

Review the five "Rs" in "Making It Personal". Discuss each one. For example, on #4 "Relate with Skill", what particular skills do your students have that can build bridges with people in the cafeteria?

(NOTE: Don't be discouraged if your students are less than enthusiastic about tackling a lunchtime ministry at school. The idea can be scary, or they may be hazy about how it can be done. Your students may imagine you're telling them to invade their lunchrooms with tracts and Bibles, buttonholing everyone they see. That's not the point. For now, simply help your students begin to tune in to needy people they see every day at lunch.)

Some students may have unusual circumstances that make lunchtime not the best time for ministry (regularly going home or running errands at lunch, for example). Help those students find different times when they have contact with people like the ones they will meet in the cafeteria. What's important is to decide on a definite, regular place and time for ministry. Lunchtime is the best.

Be prepared to answer questions on how to approach a lunchtime ministry. Build on the witnessing experiences gained in *Giving Away Your Faith*. Remind them of pointers on how to open up a conversation with someone they don't know well. Help them know how to sensitively dig more deeply into another person's life and discover what his needs are.

 APPLYING GOD'S WORD (15 minutes)
Ask your students what they wrote in the "person", "need", and "response" section on page 21.

Discuss fears students have. Be realistic about natural reservations without being negative. Let them know you're available to help and encourage them. Go to school and eat lunch with them as often as you can.

Spend time praying about these new ministries and for specific people you can help.

Assignments for Next Week: As you give the assignments on page 22 of *Influencing Your World,* express confidence that your students can and will carry out the assignments and honor their commitment to the Discipleship Group.

AFTER THE MEETING

1. Evaluate the meeting: Did students participate freely? Are they nervous about their lunchtime ministries? How can you promote positive rather than negative feelings about it? What can you do to encourage someone who is particularly scared?

2. If any group member expressed special questions or problems, phone or meet with that person this week. If the school and your schedule allow it, go to the lunchroom with students, observing and encouraging them without doing their ministry for them.

S E S S I O N   2

Step Out

OVERVIEW

Key Concept   God calls each of us to a ministry and enables us to carry out that ministry.

Memory Verse   Jeremiah 1:7

Goals   *Individual Growth:* To identify my particular ministry.

Group Life: To help each other discover our particular ministries.

BEFORE THE MEETING

1. Pray for yourself and for each group member. Ask God to continue to give you wisdom and compassion in reaching out to others.

2. In *Influencing Your World*, complete Session 2.

3. Identify your own "lunchtime" ministry (at whatever time and place is best for you), and begin looking for your own peers who have needs.

4. Memorize Jeremiah 1:7.

5. Gather materials for the meeting:
   - Bible
   - *Influencing Your World*
   - Bible memory verses
   - Telephone
   - Phone book

THE MEETING

 BUILDING THE GROUP (10 minutes)
Welcome each person warmly. Comment on things you know happened this week in students' lives.

When all students have arrived, ask for their thoughts about the lunchtime ministry you introduced last week. Give positive feedback to any who have begun to make the effort to notice people's needs. Give encouragement to any who would prefer to forget the whole thing! Share your own experience of looking around for people with needs.

FOCUSING ON LIFE (10 minutes)
Show your students the telephone and phone book. Ask: **If I wanted to call (someone's name), how would I know the number?** (Look it up in the book. In the case of a student, you would probably need to know the parent's name.) **God calls each one of us — not on the phone, but in His own unique ways. And you might say He knows your number. He knows just how to get in touch with you where you are.**

Now suppose this phone were plugged in at your home. How would you know someone was trying to call you? (it would ring) **And what would you have to do?** (answer) We can know that God is calling us through circumstances, our consciences, His Word, prayer, or our desires. He can call us and call us, but we still have to answer His call. That's what Jeremiah did.

EXPLORING GOD'S WORD (30 minutes)
Discuss the two misconceptions on page 24 of *Influencing Your World*. The second one may prompt more discussion. It can be argued either way, and endlessly, whether God has a specific will for each person's occupation in life. The point: whatever a person's occupation, God has a ministry for that person there.

Ask students to summarize what they learned about God's call in the New Testament passages on page 24.

Turn students' attention now to the first chapter of Jeremiah. Ask: **What are some things you have in common with Jeremiah at this point?** (youth; the call of God; perhaps lack of experience, and doubts) **How is it helpful to know that the great Prophet Jeremiah felt like you feel and experienced what you experience?**

Discuss some drawbacks that people often associate with being young. (lack of wisdom; lack of experience; lack of credibility with older people; Life in the teen years is sometimes considered only a "waiting period" until you get enough maturity to begin really living.) Ask: **What are some things you would like adults to know about what young people can really do?** (Encourage your students in the realization that they are important people and have much to give. God treats them as full-fledged human beings and full-fledged Christians even though they are sometimes overlooked by adults.)

Use the students' own statements about what they have to offer to counteract feelings of inadequacy they may have about their own personal ministries. Discuss the antidotes to inadequacy found in Philippians 4:13, 19.

Say: **Jeremiah was afraid when God called Him. What confidence builders did God give him? Do you need the same confidence builders? What are some specific fears you have or feelings of inadequacy about following God's call in your life?** (Fear of rejection by others and fear that the cost will be too high are two common fears. Another fear may be that of following at all because we may have misunderstood God's call and may be running in the wrong direction. That fear can paralyze us and prevent us from doing anything useful. Your students need the assurance that God can communicate His call clearly to them. Feelings of inadequacy may stem from lack of experience, knowledge, compassion, or skills.)

If you have had an experience of God confirming His call to you, such as described on page 26 of *Influencing Your World*, share it briefly with your students.

APPLYING GOD'S WORD (15 minutes)
Invite students to talk about their seven steps of confirming God's call in "Making It Personal". Let them know that they don't have to have their conclusions set in concrete for the rest of their lives, but this exercise can be an important part of the process of finding God's will for their personal ministries now. Share the excitement of young people finding out what they can do for God right now in their everyday lives, especially if a student has caught a fresh vision for how God can use him.

Pray together about your personal ministries. Pray with confidence and trust that the Lord will carry out what He has begun.

Assignments for Next Week: Make the assignments on page 33 of *Influencing Your World*. If anyone is having trouble keeping up a daily time alone with God or memorizing Scripture as assigned, offer help. You or another group member call that person once or twice this week.

AFTER THE MEETING

1. Evaluate: Are students beginning to get a vision for what God can do through them? Are some skeptical? Are some scared? Be patient with those who are holding back; not everything will happen in one week.

2. Is there a student struggling with particular feelings of inadequacy? Fear? Make an effort to phone that person or send a non-threatening note this week. Take him or her out with you to minister.

First Things First

OVERVIEW

Key Concept   Prayer is absolutely vital to our ministry of outreach.

Memory Verse   Jeremiah 33:3

Goals   *Individual Growth:* To pray habitually, regularly, and confi-
                  dently for other people.

                  Group Life: To pray with the group for people to whom
                  we want to minister.

BEFORE THE MEETING

1. Pray for each person in your Discipleship Group, including yourself.

2. In *Influencing Your World*, complete Session 3.

3. Memorize Jeremiah 33:3.

4. Gather materials for the meeting:
   - Bible
   - *Influencing Your World*
   - Bible memory verses
   - Potted plant or tree
   - Dead branch or leaf

THE MEETING

BUILDING THE GROUP (15 minutes)
After you have welcomed each person in your group, ask students to
share some of their experiences in reaching out to others at
lunchtime this week. Give all students equal praise for making a start and
for trying. Share recent ministry experiences of your own.

FOCUSING ON LIFE (10 minutes)
Show your students the potted plant or tree, and point out a particular twig or leaf. Ask: **How does it stay healthy and growing?** (It
receives water and nutrients through the the trunk and then the branches.) Ask: **What would happen if we cut off this leaf which is out on
the end?** (It would shrivel and die because it would be disconnected from
its source of life.) Show students the dead leaf or branch and ask what

happened to it. (It died because it somehow got disconnected from the main branch, and it can't live on its own.)

Have a volunteer read John 15:1-8. Discuss the main similarity between a living branch and us when we remain connected with Christ, and the similarity between a dead branch and us when we leave Christ out of our lives and ministries.

 EXPLORING GOD'S WORD (45 minutes)
Discuss: **Why would a person try to carry out a ministry in Jesus' name but forget to ask Jesus for His help with it?** (pride; ambition to accomplish something so others will think well of us; impulsiveness which doesn't want to wait on the Lord; lack of understanding of how necessary it is to depend on the Lord for success)

Prayer brings us back to our Source. When we pray, we show that we understand that any ministry we do is really Him working through us. Prayer humbles us by reminding us that without Him we can do nothing for anyone else.

Take a look at the prayer triangle based on Jeremiah 33:3 on page 35 of *Influencing Your World*. Discuss: **What is God's responsibility in the prayer triangle? In other words, what is His part? What is our responsibility? Can God be counted on to faithfully hold up His end of the arrangement? What happens when we fail to do the same? What should we do when we fail?**

Discuss the positive results of actively praying for people, even when we know that God already knows our hearts and knows what will happen. (Prayer keeps us in communication with God and changes us. It reminds us of people and their needs and keeps those people on our hearts. Prayer releases God's supernatural power. And it works! Through it God will change people.)

Discuss the promises students found in John 14-16. You might emphasize the promise of the Counselor, the Holy Spirit, who is in us and who teaches us how to pray and what to pray for. Notice also the emphasis on loving Jesus; if we love Him, our will is going to be in tune with His will, which means our prayers will be answered.

Invite students to talk about answers to prayer they have received, either very recently or in the past. The answer does not have to seem like a big thing to anyone else as long as it was a big thing between that person and God. Share one or two answered prayers of your own.

Say: **Note that having a prayer answered by the Lord does not mean dictating to God what He should do and then sitting back** while He performs it for us. We cannot tell God what to do, but we can open our hearts to Him and allow Him to reveal His will to us. Then we pray – and act – in obedience.

Discuss: **Prayer is an expression of love, and God places no limit on how far our love can go when we pray. How important is it to feel love toward the people we pray for?** (It's nice but not necessary. In fact, we may do some of our best praying when we're struggling with a person who irritates us.) **Suppose you've tried to reach out to some-body in your lunchroom and he shuts you off — even insults you. How can you pray for that person?** (Rather than praying, "Lord, show him he's wrong!" you can pray, "Lord, open his heart to me and to You. Help me be more sensitive to him and even apologize if I came on too strong." You may not feel very loving about that person, but your prayer will be in God's will.)

Share some of your good experiences of praying with others as prayer partners. Ask whether they have had similar experiences. Stress the fellow-ship and commitment between you as well as the answers to prayer.

Have students divide into threes for prayer for the people God has put on their hearts.

 APPLYING GOD'S WORD (15 minutes)
Put this chapter of *Influencing Your World* into practice right away by praying in threes for the people to whom you want to minister. Pray also for the items you named on the prayer triangle in "Making It Personal".

Remind them: **Pray specifically: let your prayers touch particular problems people have. Pray conversationally: let others offer their prayers for different requests. Pray obediently: leave your-selves open to letting God answer your prayers through you.**

Assignments for Next Week: Make the assignments on page 43 of *Influencing Your World.*

AFTER THE MEETING

1. Evaluate: Do students understand and agree that prayer is more than just an "extra" in ministry but that it is the power for ministry?

2. Are your students comfortable praying together in small groups? If any-one is having trouble, talk with that person and assure him that the intent of the heart, rather than beautiful words, is what God wants. Pray with him this week.

The Greatest Thing

OVERVIEW

Key Concept: We cannot reach out to others effectively without loving them.

Memory Verses 1 Corinthians 13:4-8a

Goals *Individual Growth:* To deepen the quality of our love for others.

Group Life: To help one another resolve unloving attitudes.

BEFORE THE MEETING

1. Pray for your group. Pray particularly for greater love among you.

2. In *Influencing Your World*, complete Session 4.

3. Memorize 1 Corinthians 13:4-8a.

4. Gather materials for the meeting:
   • Bible
   • *Influencing Your World*
   • Bible memory verses
   • Bell, gong, cymbal, or some other noisemaker with a loud, harsh sound

THE MEETING

BUILDING THE GROUP (15 minutes)
After group members have arrived and you have greeted each one, ask this question: **When did someone show real love to you?**

Give students time to think. Many experiences will be very personal and students will weigh whether or not they wish to share them. Don't worry if everybody is silent for a minute. Share your experience first to open things up.

As you and your students share your experiences of being loved, focus on these questions: **What did the person do and say? Did you feel you deserved his love? Did he make you feel you had to pay him back? How did it affect your relationship with him?**

FOCUSING ON LIFE (5 minutes)

Bring out the noisy gong, cymbal, or bell and demonstrate its loud sound. Say: **What would you do if I came up to you and started carrying on a conversation with you, all the time banging this gong so loudly you could hardly hear me? (You'd probably tell me to get lost!) With that noise the message is not clear or believable.**

Have a student read 1 Corinthians 13:1. The first verse of this great chapter on Christian love tells us that if we approach people with an unloving attitude, it doesn't matter what we say or how well we say it – people will be turned off by us as surely if we were beating a gong in their ears.

EXPLORING GOD'S WORD (45 minutes)

In Session 4 you looked at many negative effects of competition. Some students (athletes in particular) may have questions. Discuss how we can compete in athletic or scholastic realms with love.

Unloving competition is what 1 Corinthians 13 warns us against. It's an attitude of being out to win over others at their expense – socially, athletically, mentally, even spiritually! It does not care anything for the other person, only for itself. Love, in contrast, puts the other person first.

If students feel free to share their answers, discuss the results of the competition scoring you did on pages 47-51 of *Influencing Your World*. Did any of the results surprise you? Did the tests help you discover areas where your attitudes aren't what they need to be? (If the tests revealed something to you, the leader, confess it to the group and ask for their prayers as you seek to be more loving in that area.)

Discuss how each of the negative qualities of competition can stifle our efforts at ministry and turn people off.

For example, it is possible to "minister" to others competitively, trying to outdo our fellow Christians: "I witnessed to 27 people this week; I helped

Jim solve his problem with his parents." Competitiveness in ministry may be a temptation for some in your group; watch for it.

God calls us to be faithful in the work He has given us, not to be better than somebody else! If ministering to others is a competition between Christians, it will destroy our fellowship with one another and will make us obnoxious and overbearing with others. We'll minister to non-Christians not because we care about them, but because we're trying to accumulate ministry points!

Focus particularly on your students' specific problems with competition. For example, arrogance (page 48) may not be a dominant problem with many in your group, but resentment (page 51) may be one they struggle with.

Now turn students' attention to the positive by looking at the section "Love Is."

List the positive qualities of love which students found in 1 Corinthians 13. It's good to hear these things spoken aloud. Discuss: **Why do we sometimes think that being compassionate means being weak and spineless?** (A compassionate person probably comes on softer, less defensive, more open to others, and not fighting for his rights. We may have the wrong impression that it's more gutsy to stand up for yourself than to care for others and serve them.)

Ask: **What kind of strength does it take to be compassionate?** (It takes nerve to put aside our own selfish desires, courage to put up with insults or rejection from those we want to help, and self-control to be quiet and listen when we'd like to jump in with all the "right" answers. It takes patience to wait for the other person to see the truth that we think is so obvious, and to be patient with that person's negative behavior.)

Ask: **When have you seen living demonstrations of the positive qualities of love? For example, when has someone been patient with you?** (Giving real-life examples helps students see what love in action looks like.)

Ask students which of the qualities of love they have the most trouble showing to others. Discuss why these are particular problems.

As you talked about examples of love that have been shown to you, someone may have pointed out that Jesus has shown you all those good qualities of love.

Say: **Just as Jesus is the only perfect example of love, He is also the only One who can help you show each of these positive qualities of love in your life.**

For example, suppose you have trouble being patient. You can manage for a while, on the outside, but eventually your politeness wears off and you blow up in a burst of impatience. How much better to confess your lack of patience to Christ and ask Him — since He is perfectly patient — to be patient in you and through you.

APPLYING GOD'S WORD (10 minutes)
Discuss your students' findings on pages 47-51 of *Influencing Your World*: their high score averages for "Love Is Not" and their leading characteristics for "Love Is." Talk about how you can improve your love quotient, and thank God for the strong qualities of love He has put into you.

Assignments for Next Week: Make the assignments on page 58 in *Influencing Your World*.

AFTER THE MEETING

1. Evaluate: Are students seeing that love takes real strength and courage? Do any seem put off by the idea?

2. Are there any strains and tensions among members of the group? The group is an excellent place to practice Christian love. There may not be any instant cures, but try to talk with each person involved and get them together to begin to work out any problems.

NOTE: For Session 10, five weeks from now, you will need enough copies of *Following Jesus* (Book 1 in the Moving Toward Maturity series) and the *Moving Toward Maturity Series Leader's Guide* for each student to have one of each. Your students will use these books to begin to disciple younger Christians. They need to be responsible to pay for their own books and handle the money they collect from the students in their group. Contact Reach Out Youth Solutions to order the books you need.

S E S S I O N 5

Gifted Supernaturally

OVERVIEW

Key Concept God gives each of us gifts that motivate our ministries.

Memory Verses 1 Corinthians 12:4-6

Goals *Individual Growth:* To discover our spiritual gifts and begin to put them into practice.

Group Life: To help each other discover and practice our spiritual gifts.

BEFORE THE MEETING

1. Pray for everyone in your group (yourself included) that the Lord will show each of you the particular gifts He has given you.

2. In *Influencing Your World*, complete Session 5.

3. If you have not considered your own spiritual gifts before, or if you are uncertain what they are, think, pray, and study about them this week. Ask people close to you what they believe your spiritual gifts are.

4. Memorize 1 Corinthians 12:4-6.

5. Gather materials for the meeting:
   - Bible
   - *Influencing Your World*
   - Bible memory verses
   - Wrapped gift for each person (Make it something inexpensive but desirable, such as a candy bar, and disguise it by using a large or odd-shaped box.)

THE MEETING

BUILDING THE GROUP (15 minutes)
Welcome each person in a special way this week by letting each one know how much you value him or her.

Give students time to talk together about their lunchtime ministries. Some may have encouraging things to share with the group. Others may have questions about how to handle a problem or a question which a non-Christian has brought up. Still others may be discouraged at seeing no immediate results. Show your students that they are doing God's will whether or not others respond.

FOCUSING ON LIFE (10 minutes)
Show your students the wrapped gifts and ask whether anyone would like to receive a present. Some may be willing, and others may be more hesitant. Ask the hesitant ones: **What makes you hesitate to accept this gift? Are you afraid of what might be inside? Do you think it might not really be for you?** Discuss what makes us willing or unwilling to receive a gift.

Offer a gift to one person. If that person doesn't take it, select another person and so on until someone takes the gift and opens it.

Say: **God gives us all kinds of gifts such as life, health, and family. But the Scriptures tell us about a special kind of gift, spiritual gifts, that are given particularly for ministry to others. But we have to take those gifts and open them.** Give each person in the group a gift.

EXPLORING GOD'S WORD (30 minutes)
Discuss: **What do we usually think when we say that a person is "gifted"?** (He or she has special natural abilities. How is that different from having spiritual gifts? Anyone, Christian or non-Christian, can have natural, God-given gifts or talents. They can be used in many different ways to get ahead, to make money, to impress other people. They can also be used unselfishly, to serve others. But a spiritual gift is not a natural ability. It is a God-given capacity for service through which the Holy Spirit ministers to others.)

Discuss the motivations, ministries, and manifestations on pages 64-65 of *Influencing Your World*.

Ask whether students have any particular questions about spiritual gifts. Some may never have considered this topic before. Point them back to the Scriptures in this session. If you have gone through a process of discovering and using your spiritual gift, share that with your students now. Reassure your students that as they pray and learn more, God will reveal their spiritual gifts to them. As they seek God, the gifts will become clear.

Discuss how some of the gifts can come into play as you minister to others. For example, how can the gift of encouragement, or exhortation, be a practical help to somebody this week? What about the gift of giving? How could these gifts come into play this week in the school lunchroom?

Ask students what they think their gifts might be. Invite other students to give their reactions positively. For example, if Elizabeth believes her gift is prophecy, someone might respond, "I can agree with that. Elizabeth helps us see when we're on the wrong track and puts us back in a loving way." Say: **A person might see in himself things he would like to do rather than what God actually enables him to do! For instance, a bossy person might think he has the gift of leadership. Our true spiritual gifts will be found through seeking God in prayer, practically experimenting with our gifts and allowing others to confirm the gift. If nobody else thinks you have the spiritual gift you think you have, you should take another look at your gifts and ask God to show you the truth.**

 **APPLYING GOD'S WORD** (15 minutes)
Assuming that you have an idea of what your spiritual gifts for ministry are, make plans together to put them into practice in your individual and group ministries. This can be an exciting new experience for people who are discovering gifts they didn't know they had.

Assignments for Next Week: Make the assignments on page 70 in *Influencing Your World*.

AFTER THE MEETING

1. Evaluate: Are students catching an exciting glimpse of what God can do through the use of their spiritual gifts? Are some students still doubtful or confused? Meet with any students who seem confused.

2. Did students respond positively and lovingly to each other's thoughts on their own spiritual gifts?

S E S S I O N   6

With a Towel

OVERVIEW

Key Concept We have the privilege of serving others when we follow Jesus.

Memory Verses John 13:14-15

Goals *Individual Growth:* To find ways to serve other people.

Group Life: To find ways to serve one another.

BEFORE THE MEETING

1. Pray for yourself and each of your students. An attitude of serving does not come easily or naturally. It must come from Christ, the greatest servant.

2. In *Influencing Your World*, complete Session 5.

3. Memorize John 13:14-15.

4. Gather materials for the meeting:
   • Bible
   • *Influencing Your World*
   • Bible memory verses
   • Towel
   • Container of water

THE MEETING

BUILDING THE GROUP (15 minutes)
Welcome each person warmly. Remember that you are this group's servant. God has already given you many opportunities to serve students, and there will be many more opportunities.

This would be a good time to review some of your conclusions about your spiritual gifts (from last week's session). Ask students whether they have any new thoughts about what their gifts are and whether they have tried to put their gifts into practice this week.

FOCUSING ON LIFE (30 minutes)
Display the towel and ask students what it can be used for. Though there are many possible uses for a towel, students will think of "foot-washing" or "service".

Ask students if they would be willing to wash one another's feet. Notice if they balk or seem turned off. Say: **Even though you are friends — and fairly clean when you arrived at this meeting — the idea of lowering ourselves to wash one another's feet is not very attractive. Jesus calls us to wash the feet, not only of our nice clean friends, but the feet of unattractive and ungrateful people. Like the impossible standard of love in 1 Corinthians 13 (Session 4), this standard of service is impossible without love from our example, the master servant, Jesus.**

Create a quiet, reverent atmosphere is which members of your Discipleship Group can actually wash each other's feet. You begin by washing someone's feet and letting others do the same. Do it humbly, without talking. This can be a moving experience for your group and a memorable illustration of a servant's humble spirit.

Lead your group in a discussion of what they learned from this experience. Hang up the towel in your meeting room tonight where everyone can see it, as a symbol of service. You may even wish to leave it there as a continued reminder.

EXPLORING GOD'S WORD (35 minutes)
Ask: **How does our society teach us to be selfish?**
(Advertisements tell us to indulge ourselves by buying more and better things. Many expressions such as "Do yourself a favor," "I'm looking out for #1," "I owe it to myself," "I've got to take care of me" fill our everyday language. It is simply assumed that you will look for the degree and the job that will bring in the most money, the most prestige, the most pleasure. If you give your life to serve others, you will be out of step with our times. People may even question your motives.)

Discuss: **What can we do to counteract all the pressures that tell us to be selfish?** (We can make an effort to tune out the clamor by concentrating on what God wants for us instead. For example, when the slick and persuasive ads come on, we don't have to sit like zombies and absorb them! We can hit the remote.) **Action follows the heart, and to live counter to society we must act. What we do and where we invest our interest and attention will show where our hearts are. If you act as a servant — even when you don't feel like it — you will become a servant. Investing in other people's needs makes you other-centered rather than self-centered.**

Turn to John 13. We know from Luke 22:24 that the disciples had been arguing about who was the biggest and best follower of Jesus. Ask: **What struggles might have been going on inside the Son of God as He got up and took that towel and basin to wash their feet?** (He could easily have wanted to reprimand them harshly. He was about to die and He needed their comfort and friendship, not their bickering. He may not have wanted to serve them. He must have been very lonely as He took up that servant's towel and began to do what none of His disciples understood.)

How can Jesus' struggle help us as we serve others? (Serving was not always fun for Jesus, and it won't always be fun for us. But God will bless us, as John 13:17 says.)

Discuss: **If you were God and you wanted to show people you were God and what God is like, what do you think you would do?** (Students will have all kinds of answers. From our human perspective we would expect God to create lightning bolts or crush some buildings to show off His power.) **How did Jesus show what God is like?** (He took the lowest role of a servant.) Read Philippians 2:5-8 to see how Jesus humbled Himself to show us what the serving heart of God is like.

Find out what else the group has discovered from the Scriptures about being servants (page 74).

What benefits come to us when we take the position of a servant? (letting go of the need to protect and defend yourself all the time — looking out for number one can get to be a chore; knowing you're in God's will and doing what is close to His heart; seeing others benefit by what you do; feeling fulfilled)

Describe the rewards you, the leader, have received from serving. (We benefit not only from the short-term emotional benefits, but also from the long-term benefits of development of our character.)

What are some of our "comfort zones"? (anything that protects us from meeting other people's needs; routine; the same close circle of friends; responsibilities that keep us too busy) Even this Discipleship Group can become a comfort zone if we lose our vision and focus.

What do we need to "lay aside" to serve others? (Answers will be different for each person.)

Serving is a terrific idea in the abstract and theoretical. But actually getting in there and doing it can be tough. What reservations do you have about that? (Discuss reactions such as those mentioned and others students may be experiencing about being servants.)

Review the promise of John 13:17. **Think of some ways that you have been blessed when you served others.** (Ask students to describe those blessings.) **Let's count on God to bless us in ways we never dreamed possible!**

APPLYING GOD'S WORD (10 minutes)
Pray for one another as you look forward to opportunities to serve this week. You can serve each other by praying for each other tonight and all week. Ask God to show you specific things you can do to serve others. They may not seem like a big deal to you, but they will be significant to the people you serve and will show those people the love of God.

Assignments for Next Week: Complete the assignments on pages 80 of *Influencing Your World*.

AFTER THE MEETING

1. Evaluate: Are students looking forward to depending on God in the area of serving others? Are some scared of the idea of getting in the middle of somebody else's problems?

2. If someone has a special struggle, find a way to serve that person in his struggle this week.

S E S S I O N   7

No Limits

OVERVIEW

Key Concept   We can develop generosity as we learn to give money away.

Memory Verse   2 Corinthians 9:6-7

Goals   *Individual Growth:* To discover the blessing of managing money in order to give it away.

                    Group Life: To encourage each other to handle money in a way that pleases God.

BEFORE THE MEETING

1. Pray for everyone in your group, asking the Lord to build a generous spirit in your students.

2. In *Influencing Your World,* complete Session 7.

3. Think about your own experience with managing money and giving it to the Lord. Do you have personal financial issues that are not resolved? Have you found workable solutions to budgeting, tithing, and being in debt? Be prepared to share these with your students where applicable to their situations.

4. Memorize 2 Corinthians 9:6-7.

5. Gather materials for the meeting:
   - Bible
   - *Influencing Your World*
   - Bible memory verses
   - Towel (from last week's session)
   - Budget records of your own (if they are organized and clear enough to help your students make their own budgets)

THE MEETING

BUILDING THE GROUP (15 minutes)
After welcoming everyone, hang up the "towel of service" from last

week's session and ask your students how their experiences of serving worked out this week. Invite volunteers to tell about any experiences, big or small, they had in trying to serve others. Tell about anything that has happened to you in serving this week. Affirm your students for any efforts at service, no matter how small, and encourage them to continue.

FOCUSING ON LIFE (10 minutes)
Say: **When Jesus took up the towel on the night of the Last Supper, He served His disciples by washing their feet. And He was about to serve all mankind by dying on the cross. He gave His service and His life freely. Read 2 Corinthians 8:9. Jesus lived a life of giving rather than getting. Giving includes many things - time, abilities, attention, a listening ear, and money.**

Discuss briefly: **Why is it hard for many people to part with their money even to an obvious and legitimate need right in front of them?** (Money is precious because it means "power" in our culture; it buys us things we enjoy; it spells security for the future.)

Discuss: **God *can* meet people's needs directly, by dropping food or clothes from the sky, for example. Why do you think He avoids that approach and instead asks us to give to people in need?** (Because it builds character, puts us in contact with real people who have real needs, teaches us to let go of worldly security, and provides the opportunity for God to meet our needs.)

EXPLORING GOD'S WORD (45 minutes)
Say: **Prepare a list of everything God has given to you. You cannot possibly list everything, but come up with as much as you can. You could continue to list all night and not be finished so stop after page one.**

Is God a giver? You bet He is! And since He is our example, He naturally asks us to be givers too. The point is not that God has given us so much that we should feel guilty if we don't give, but that we are more like Christ when we give to others.

Someone might say that it doesn't cost God anything to give what He has given, while it hurts me in the wallet when I give. But the gift of His Son cost Him His greatest treasure (John 3:16).

Read 2 Corinthians 9:6-11. **What is the tone or mood of this pas-**

sage? Is it saying, "Give, because God will zap you if you don't"? No, it has a positive and cheerful tone. It's saying, "God will bless you when you give."

Discuss the kinds of blessings God gives us when we give to others. (It's not necessarily a guarantee of being paid back materially, although God may do that; it may be the blessings of feeling useful, knowing we've helped someone, feeling free of the grip of money, peace in obeying God, joy in becoming like Christ.)

How does giving to others help us grow as Christians? (we have to trust God more to provide for us; we obey Him, which always helps us grow; we take Him at His word instead of relying on our feelings; we discover that He is faithful to us; we imitate Christ)

What are the scriptural uses of money? (It is a legitimate means of exchange, and we don't have to feel guilty about using it to buy what we need or to provide for family members who count on us for support. The wise use and investment of money can provide us with a means of saving and meeting emergencies. But money is also meant to help us learn to be generous. One of the reasons we have it is so we can give it away!)

What are some advantages of having a planned system of giving rather than doing it hit-and-miss as you hear about needs? (The hit-and-miss method may seem more spiritual to some people because it is spontaneous and seems to rely on God's moment-by-moment leading. But it can easily be based on emotions rather than the Holy Spirit's prompting. When we give to causes that move us the most at the time, we're subject to the most emotional and well-packaged appeal that happens to come in the mail right then. A definite plan of giving, made out objectively ahead of time, takes away that unreliable element of emotionalism.)

Think of a time when someone has been generous to you. How did you feel about the person? How did it affect your relationship? How does giving help your relationships as well as help meet physical needs? (NOTE: *How* a gift is given can affect a relationship for good or bad. Perhaps someone has been "generous" to you but makes it clear that something is expected in return, either materially or in unending gratitude! Giving in the right spirit, expecting nothing back, will help rather than harm our relationships. Of course, there is always the danger that people will misunderstand our motives. But even Jesus took that risk and was misunderstood by many, so we can't expect to be any different.)

How can we begin to put giving into practice, if we aren't in the habit already? (You may want to mention how you began to tithe and/or to give to those in need, how God showed you the importance of giving, and how He has blessed you as a result.)

Ask students about the results of their budget-making. Show them your own budget if you have brought it to the meeting. Of course, your financial situation and that of your students living with their parents are probably quite different, but they need to know that having money requires a plan for using it.

(NOTE: You will have to make many allowances for students' differing financial situations. You will have students who work and must provide for many of their own needs, other students whose parents give them whatever they want, and everything in between. But students need to be aware of the money they spend — no matter where it comes from — and plan their spending. Each person receives X amount of money and needs to spend Y amount of money. Each person needs to learn to give a portion of his money for God's purposes.)

APPLYING GOD'S WORD (20 minutes)
As a demonstration of drawing up a workable budget, ask for a student volunteer to present his or her financial picture, or make up a fictional student as an example. Work together as a group to help that student draw up a budget. Discuss each item and come to conclusions together. (The student does not have to feel bound by the group's decisions, but the exercise should be helpful to the entire group.)

Assignments for Next Week: Complete the assignments on page 93 in *Influencing Your World*.

AFTER THE MEETING

1. Evaluate: Do students seem to feel freedom about giving money for the Lord? Does it make them uptight?

2. Was any student made uncomfortable because he didn't have as much money as the others? If you have an opportunity this week, try to give that student reassurance that everyone in the group is equal in God's eyes and in your eyes.

(NOTE: Have you ordered enough copies of *Following Jesus* and the *Moving Toward Maturity Series Leader's Guide* for each student to have one? They will need these for Session 10, two weeks from now.)

S E S S I O N   8

In the Dirt

OVERVIEW

Key Concept   Serving others brings inconvenience and cost, but also rewards.

Memory Verses   Matthew 22:37-39

Goals   *Individual Growth:* To become more willing to take risks in serving people.

Group Life: To encourage ministry to needy people.

BEFORE THE MEETING

1. Pray for each person in your Discipleship Group.

2. Pray for needy people you know – especially people who need someone to care.

3. In *Influencing Your World*, complete Session 8.

4. Memorize Matthew 22:37-39.

5. Gather materials for the meeting:
   - Bible
   - *Influencing Your World*
   - Bible memory verses

NOTE: Arrange to arrive at this meeting with dirty hands. It should be dirt that will rub off on other people but will also wash off easily, such as dirt from a garden.

THE MEETING

BUILDING THE GROUP (15 minutes)

As people arrive, greet them enthusiastically by shaking hands firmly with your dirty hands. Watch people's reactions as they realize they have just gotten dirty by shaking hands with you. After everyone has arrived, ask: **How did you feel about getting dirty by shaking hands with me?** Discuss people's reactions. Take time for everyone to wash their hands before you continue.

FOCUSING ON LIFE (10 minutes)
Ask your freshly washed group: **Suppose I came to the group dirty – for real. It wasn't just an exercise. How would you respond to me?**

Helping people in trouble may not mean getting dirty physically — though it sometimes means that too — but it always means risk-taking and inconvenience. Yet the rewards are great for us and for the people we help.

EXPLORING GOD'S WORD (35 minutes)
Look at Luke 10:25-37. **What answer do you think the lawyer was hoping for when he asked, "And who is my neighbor?" (v. 29)** (probably someone respectable and easy to care about)

Why do you suppose Jesus answered by telling this long story? (He often answered that way to disarm people. People naturally let their guard down when they listen to a story. Jesus would introduce a situation or principle in a story and tell it so people would agree with Him, whether they wanted to or not.)

What kinds of wounded, hurting people do you come in contact with every day? Why are those wounds harder to notice than the injuries of the man who was robbed on the road to Jericho?

Have you ever felt hurt and wounded, and watched people ignore you? Describe how you felt.

Potentially we risk our reputations when we befriend a needy person. How will you handle that? (You will have to decide if helping a hurting person is worth the risk of giving others a bad impression of you. Will you actually harm your witness, or will you just give negative people a chance to gossip about you? Can you trust God to take care of your reputation as you serve others?)

What other risks do we take when we help people in need? (losing time; losing popularity; getting distracted from our own ambitions; being thought of as "different"; getting physically hurt in some cases)

What risks did the Samaritan take when he stopped to help the robbery victim? (being robbed himself; losing time; having to spend money even if it wasn't stolen from him; being inconvenienced in several ways, such as having to walk)

Discuss: **What difficulties are you having in letting your compas-**

sion flow freely toward needy people?" (Encourage the group to open their hearts and share honestly.)

Talk about specific actions you can take to show compassion to people. Notice how seemingly small some of the Samaritan's actions were – like going over to the injured man and touching him. Our small gestures can be life-saving for a person in need. Just stopping where that injured man lay was more than anybody else had done for him all day!

What makes us unwilling to inconvenience ourselves for people? What does that say about our values — what's important to us? (For example, if I don't have time to give an unpopular person a ride home from school when he's loaded down with books because I have to go play tennis, then tennis is more important to me than helping people. It's not that I shouldn't play tennis, or that I have to give everybody I pass a ride home; but it does tell me something about my values.)

Galatians 6:9 says, "Let us not become weary in doing good." Discuss: **Have you grown weary in your lunchtime ministry these past weeks? How does this week's session encourage you to keep on serving?** (Talk about it openly.) Review the promise in the second half of that verse: "for at the proper time we will reap a harvest if we do not give up."

APPLYING GOD'S WORD (15 minutes)
Give students the opportunity to consider specific things they will do this week to show compassion for specific people who need help. Let them share ideas with those who are having trouble coming up with something — finding the courage to do it! Pray together for the people you want to help, for opportunities to help them, and for willingness and courage to help them.

Assignments for Next Week: Make the assignments on pages 106 in *Influencing Your World.*

AFTER THE MEETING

1. Evaluate: Are students turned on or turned off by the idea of deliberately "getting their hands dirty" ministering to others?

2. Is one of your own students an "untouchable" who needs a special touch from you or from another student this week?

S E S S I O N   9

Multiply Your Life

OVERVIEW

Key Concept   We can multiply God's kingdom by discipling others.

Memory Verse   2 Timothy 2:2

Goals   *Individual Growth:* To begin selecting people to disciple and understand how to disciple them.

Group Life: To support each other in the responsibility of discipling others.

BEFORE THE MEETING

1. Pray for each member of your Discipleship Group.

2. Think about how you have gone about discipling your students. What has gone particularly well? What could you have done better? (Your leadership of this Discipleship Group has been your students' chief example of what it means to disciple younger Christians.)

3. In *Influencing Your World,* complete Session 9.

4. Memorize 2 Timothy 2:2.

5. Gather materials for the meeting:
   - Bible
   - *Influencing Your World*
   - Bible memory verses
   - Paper
   - *Following Jesus* and *Moving Toward Maturity Series Leader's Guide* – one copy of each for each student

THE MEETING

BUILDING THE GROUP (15 minutes)
As students arrive, greet each one with clean hands this week!

Hand out paper and tell students to write their names at the top of the sheet. Collect the sheets of paper, turn them over, and mix them up. Hand them out again face down and give students these instructions: **Write a message to the person whose name appears on your paper. Express one way in which he is a good example to you. For example: "Kevin Peterson, you're an example of cheerfulness even when things aren't going well." Or, "Maria Williams, your sportsmanship in volleyball is a good example to all of us poor losers." Don't sign what you write. Hand your papers back. I'll distribute them at the end of our meeting.**

Collect the papers and save them for the end of the meeting.

FOCUSING ON LIFE (15 minutes)
Ask students: **Who has modeled following Jesus to you?** Ask what students saw in those people and how those people demonstrated faith in Christ.

(If students mention you, the leader — great! If they don't mention your name, don't be crushed; they may be too shy to say it to your face. You can be confident that if you have faithfully and prayerfully led this Discipleship Group, you have been a good example to your students.)

EXPLORING GOD'S WORD (35 minutes)
As students consider taking on the task of discipling younger Christians, ask them what their feelings, hopes, and fears might be. To some it may look like an impossible task. They may say, "Who am I to try to teach somebody else? I've had trouble getting through my own assignments every week." Help them voice these feelings out loud in front of each other. Express confidence that they can do it, no matter how inadequate they feel.

Share with your students any feelings of inadequacy you had as you began this or an earlier Discipleship Group. If you still have feelings of inadequacy, tell students about that too. Rather than lowering yourself in their eyes, you'll be an example of honesty — and how God can use a person who doesn't feel adequate, if that person is willing to obey anyway.

Discuss: **What can you do well now, but you felt inadequate to do when you began?** (Nearly any learned skill or sport works that way.) **How can you apply that experience to beginning to disciple other Christians?** (If you try and keep trying, pick yourself up when you fail, and learn all you can along the way, you'll succeed!)

Discuss: **Do you think you have to be fully mature in Christ in order to teach somebody else?** Notice the definition of "making disciples" on page 109 of *Influencing Your World*. It is "one maturing believer" — not a perfect believer — "reproducing other maturing believers." If we wait until we are perfect before we try to help anybody else, we will never do anything helpful. God calls imperfect people to disciple other imperfect people.

Why is it important to stay close to Christ as we begin discipling others? Read John 15:5 together. (Apart from Jesus, we can do nothing. We may be able to recite a lot of Bible facts, but we won't help anybody grow as a Christian because we won't have real spiritual power flowing through us.)

Discuss how to go about approaching someone you think you would like to disciple. **To whom could you simply say, "I'd like to get together with you regularly and study the Bible and talk about Christ"?** (You could approach a younger Christian friend with whom you already have a close relationship.) Ask students to think of potential disciples.

Often the best approach is to initially leave out the word disciple. The student can simply ask a younger Christian if he would like to get together to talk about his relationship with Christ, using *Following Jesus* to focus the time.

As you take a younger Christian under your wing and begin to spend time with him or her, what attitude will help you? (love; caring about the best interests of the person; sensitivity to the person's feelings; a listening ear; firmness in helping the person keep his commitment; belief in the person's full potential, not having an inflated idea of our own importance, overprotectiveness of the person, ego involvement in how well the person "succeeds" as a Christian, or a critical attitude)

Tell your students how you go about trying to be "real" with them. What are some advantages of letting students see your faults? Give students the opportunity to tell you what they've learned by seeing you, their leader, make mistakes. (When you're "real" with those you're trying to teach, you show them by example that a Christian is not perfect, but forgiven; that God loves us when we fail; that God will pick us up again no matter how many times we fall down.)

What causes us not to be "real" with people? (fear of what people will think, fear they'll reject us, fear we'll damage the Lord's reputation by hurting our witness — But a phony witness is no witness at all!)

What can happen as people in this Discipleship Group take on younger Christians and begin to help them grow? (Let students tell their dreams of what God can do through them. They can change people's lives, change their class, change their school for Christ!)

 APPLYING GOD'S WORD (15 minutes)
Hand out the copies of *Following Jesus* and *the Moving Toward Maturity Series Leader's Guide*. (Discuss payment as you wish.) Since your students went through *Following Jesus* some time ago, they may enjoy reviewing the course. Talk about how they can use *Following Jesus* and the other books in the Moving Toward Maturity series to disciple others. See pages 118-120 of *Influencing Your World* for suggestions.

Give students the opportunity to talk about people they want to disciple. Let them make suggestions to one another. You need to have communication among you to prevent five people from descending on one person whom they have all decided is "their" disciple!

Pray for the people you are considering as potential disciples. Ask God to show each of you whom you should disciple and to confirm or revise any choices made.

As students leave, give them their "good example" sheets.

Assignments for Next Week: Make the assignments on pages 120 in *Influencing Your World*.

The next session is the final meeting of this Discipleship Group! Plan something special for your last time together. Be creative. Make it really fun!

AFTER THE MEETING

1. Evaluate: Do your students believe they can disciple others effectively? Do they understand how to use *Following Jesus*?

2. Does someone need extra encouragement from you this week?

NOTE: In Session 10, your students are instructed to consider their priorities in ministry and discuss these with you. This week phone or meet with each student and discuss this matter with him or her. (See pages 125-126 of *Influencing Your World*.)

SESSION 10

From Here to There

OVERVIEW

Key Concept   Prayerful planning will maximize ministry.

Memory Verse   Matthew 10:42

Goals   *Individual Growth:* To decide on ministry priorities and plans.

                  Group Life: To continue your group ministry projects.

BEFORE THE MEETING

1. Pray for everyone in your Discipleship Group. Thank God for each person's growth and the fellowship you experienced. Pray for ongoing, growing ministries for each one.

2. In *Influencing Your World*, do Session 10.

3. Toward the end of the week, phone each student to inquire about his or her ministry priorities (see pages 125-126 of *Influencing Your World*).

4. Memorize Matthew 10:42.

5. Gather materials for the meeting:
   - Bible
   - *Influencing Your World*
   - Bible memory verses

THE MEETING

BUILDING THE GROUP (20 minutes)
Make this a time of expressing your special appreciation to your Discipleship Group. Tell each one specifically how he has helped you grow, as well as how you've seen him grow. Give your students the opportunity to tell what this Discipleship Group has meant to them. If you have planned refreshments, enjoy them together during this time.

FOCUSING ON LIFE (10 minutes)
Discuss: **What in your future do you have no control over?**

(the economy; international conflicts which might mean being called into military service; parents' job changes; friends becoming fickle; college loans becoming less available; death) **What in your future do you have at least some control over?** (your attitude toward what happens; how hard you study to get the best school record possible; how well you perform your job; how faithful you remain to Christ and the church; how you perform your ministry)

Our lives change. We can't foresee where we will be in the future. But we can decide that no matter where we are or what we are doing, we will have a ministry to someone.

 EXPLORING GOD'S WORD (45 minutes)
Discuss: **Sometimes Christians think that the more Christian activities they are involved in, the greater their ministry is. How can good activities, even church activities, harm our real ministries?** (They can run us ragged. They can distract us from people by concentrating on activities and programs. They can keep us surrounded by other Christians so we are insulated from non-Christians who need us. They keep us too busy.)

How can we choose among all the opportunities available to us and decide where we actually belong in Christ's service? (prayerfully following God's plan, as analyzed in Matthew 10 in this chapter of *Influencing Your World,* and refusing to jump into everything that comes along without carefully considering God's will)

Why is it vital to know we are called to Jesus rather than to a job, church, cause, or anything else? (Jobs, youth groups, popular causes, and ministry organizations can all break down and disintegrate, leaving their participants disappointed and wondering what happened. Many Christians, deeply committed to a particular ministry, flounder when that ministry fails them. They feel abandoned by God. But God calls us to Himself first, and then He will use us in some ministry of His choosing for as long as He chooses.)

What happens when we try to minister to too many people in too many places at once? (We get burned out. We short-change everybody and water down the good that we could accomplish if we had concentrated on fewer people. We can't compare ourselves with each other in this; some people have more time and energy than others; some are gifted in one-on-one ministry while others are better with large groups.)

Discuss: **What steps have you gone through to narrow down your ministry priorities?** (You should have talked with each of your students about this during the week. Let them share their decisions now.)

During these weeks of studying personal ministry, have you changed your mind about what your ministry is or come to any surprising conclusions about how God might want you to minister? (Discuss new insights students have reached.)

How can we have a definite plan for future ministry and yet stay open to God's surprises? (Plan what you can and commit yourself, but don't worry about changing your directions as God leads you. Keep in mind that no ministry is sacred; only God is perfect and holy.)

Share together the "Practical Ministry Plans" your students have come up with (page 132 of *Influencing Your World*). Help each other make realistic but risk-taking plans for future ministry. Discuss how you can help each other carry out your plans, remembering that each person's plan is also individual and his responsibility.

 APPLYING GOD'S WORD (15 minutes)
Celebrate your final meeting together as a Discipleship Group by praying and worshipping together and encouraging each other in your future ministries. If you need to talk about continuing your group ministry project, this would be a good time to plan and pray further about that.

Try to talk with each person before he leaves. Affirm each one for his or her faithfulness.

Carry out your creative fun activity!

No assignments

The Complete Moving Toward Maturity Series

A six book progressive discipleship series that will move students to spiritual maturity in Christ

GETTING STARTED helps new believers successfully begin their walk with Christ.

FOLLOWING JESUS builds a solid foundation for a life-changing relationship with Christ and for becoming a disciple of Christ.

SPENDING TIME ALONE WITH GOD deepens students' relationship with Jesus by learning how to spend time with Him.

MAKING JESUS LORD challenges students to obey Jesus and give Him control in the day-to-day issues they face.

GIVING AWAY YOUR FAITH guides students on the wild adventure of overcoming their fears and taking the risk to boldly communicate Christ.

INFLUENCING YOUR WORLD shows students that they can become influential leaders through serving the needs of the people around them.

TIME ALONE WITH GOD NOTEBOOK gives students practical tools for guiding them in their adventure with God.

LEADER'S GUIDE gives the group leader all the reasons needed to lead a lively and life-changing discipleship group. This book contains the leader's material from all five books of the Moving Toward Maturity series

MOVING TOWARD MATURITY REFERENCE KIT contains all of the Moving Toward Maturity books plus six tapes designed to inspire you as a discipler of students.

For these and other books and resources:
Order online at **www.reach-out.org**
or by phone: **1-800-473-9456**

Moving Toward Maturity Leader's Resources

LEADER'S GUIDE

What do I need to disciple students? Passion for God, love for kids, and this Leader's Guide! All of the resources you need to relate to your students, prepare for your group, and lead interactive, lively and life-changing discussions are in your hand. This book contains the leader's material for the five books in the Moving Toward Maturity series.

AUDIO KIT

The Audio Kit offers discipleship group leaders motivation for discipling students. Speakers Louie Giglio, Dave Busby and Barry St. Clair do not offer step-by-step instruction, instead, they prepare and inspire discipleship leaders at the heart level.

LEADER'S RESOURCE KIT

The Moving Toward Maturity Resource Kit contains all of the Moving Toward Maturity books plus six tapes designed to inspire you as a discipler of students.

For these and other books and resources:
Order online at **www.reach-out.org**
or by phone: **1-800-473-9456**

Jesus No Equal
A Passionate Encounter with the Son of God

This student devotional creates an intense encounter with Jesus that traces Christ's coming, His birth, life, ministry, death, resurrection, and second coming. The challenge of this book is for students to spend at least 20 minutes a day discovering Jesus. They will come to know Jesus for who He really is and will follow Him more passionately. That encounter will create the enthusiasm they need to take Jesus to their schools with the good news that in Jesus there is no equal. This book is much more than a resource. It is a campaign to place Jesus at center stage in the lives of the younger generation.

Leader's Guide
This six-session leader's guide is an in depth discipling resource that helps the group leader equip students to intimately know and walk with Jesus. Each session contains interactive activities, timely, relevant illustrations, video clip suggestions, and powerful small group discussion questions.

Audio Set
These five messages by Barry St. Clair make Jesus so real and so relevant to students that they will be motivated to have the same passion for Jesus that Barry has!

Booklet
The *Jesus No Equal* booklet explains the heart of the life-changing message of Jesus to students. It's design will help Christian students communicate Christ to their non-believing friends.

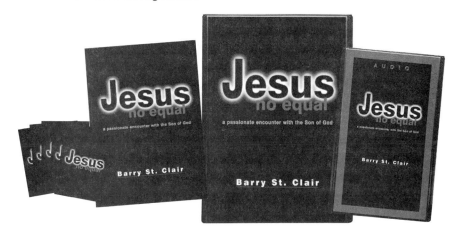

For this and other books and resources:
Order online at www.reach-out.org or by phone: 1-800-473-9456

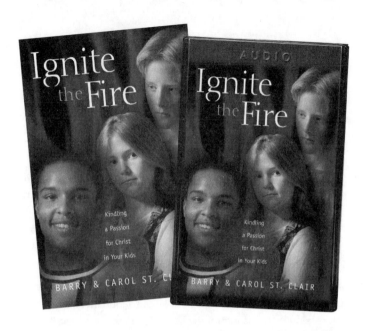

IGNITE THE FIRE
Kindling a Passion for Christ in Your Kids

Barry and Carol St. Clair raised four children who are living proof of the message of this book. The circumstances that brought this book into existence are compelling – a couple who loved each other, parents who placed Jesus in the center of their home, children who responded to love and discipline, and their mother who died while the book was being written.

Most parents ask the question: "What can I do to help my children turn out right?" In *Ignite the Fire*, Barry and Carol suggest a better question: "What can I do help my children love Jesus more?" This book offers ten Christ-centered actions that parents can take to help motivate their children to pursue Jesus.

AUDIO SET — Barry St. Clair challenges parents to see that their kids will be passionate about what they are passionate about. Since parenting is mostly a matter of the heart, then grace, not rules, will cause kids to love Jesus. Parents, not the church, have a primary privilege of discipling their kids and their kids' friends. With an environment of passion, grace and discipleship, biblical discipline will positively shape our kids' lives.

For this and other books and resources:
Order online at www.reach-out.org or by phone: 1-800-473-9456

Penetrating the Campus
How To Reach Students Where They Are

Designed to equip youth leaders to know how to relate to young people on their turf, this book helps leaders understand non-believing students. As students face the emotional, social, and spiritual challenges of adolescence and of life on their middle school or high school campuses, youth leaders can "be there" to influence students' lives.

In *Penetrating the Campus,* Barry St. Clair and Keith Naylor give youth pastors, volunteer leaders, and parents in-depth, practical advice for communicating God's love to high school students. This book helps youth leaders bridge the gap between their church ministry and the public school campus — probably the most important mission field in America today.

For this and other books and resources:
Order online at www.reach-out.org or by phone: 1-800-473-9456

The Magnet Effect

You can attract non-believing students to hear the Gospel. *The Magnet Effect* will show you how!

In *The Magnet Effect* book and video, Barry St. Clair teams with the Willow Creek Youth Ministry Team to challenge youth leaders to create events designed to draw non-believing students to Christ.

The Magnet Effect book offers simple yet powerful strategies and tools for outreach. These strategies and tools enable youth leaders to equip their students for involvement in outreach opportunities that will help them reach their friends for Christ. The Magnet Effect gives step-by-step plans for selecting and preparing adult volunteers and student teams, developing a publicity plan, preparing a realistic budget, hosting the event, and doing effective follow-up. Included also is an Outreach Event Planner that walks the leaders through the entire process.

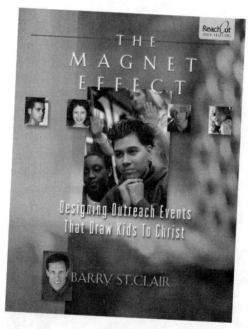

The Magnet Effect video illustrates an excellent outreach event.

This set is an essential tool for youth ministries that want to reach students.

For this and other books and resources:
Order online at www.reach-out.org or by phone: 1-800-473-9456

Jesus-Focused Youth Ministry

This Jesus-focused approach to youth ministry creates an environment of powerful prayer and then builds on 5 Core Principles within that environment. Church based and campus oriented, this strategy answers these questions based on the principles that Jesus used in His ministry:

Going Deeper with Christ – How do you develop intimacy in your relationship to Jesus and reflect Him to others?

Building Leaders – How do you build quality leaders for a long-term ministry?

Discipling Students – How do you disciple students to have spiritual passion and become spiritual influencers with their friends?

Penetrating the Culture – How do you motivate and mobilize your leaders and students to penetrate the student culture?

Creating Outreach Opportunities – How do you design outreach opportunities for students to reach their non-believing friends?

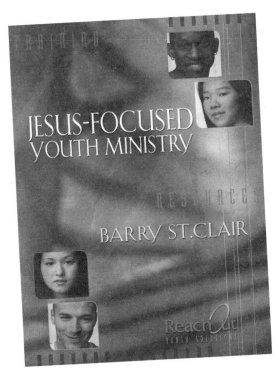

For this and other books and resources:
Order online at www.reach-out.org or by phone: 1-800-473-9456

Life Happens— Get Ready

Do you think deciding what to do on Saturday is a long-range plan? That's normal. But the "biggies" will be decided in the next five years: college, job, lifelong friends, marriage partner (really scary!) That's why you need to answer these huge questions now: who am I? where am I going? how am I going to get there? *Life Happens* provides you with nine practical "destiny deciders" to help you discover God's unique destiny for your life. Spend a few minutes a day reading and writing in *LIfe Happens* and you'll start to see the fantastic life God has in store for you.

Taking Your Campus For Christ

Now that's a radical idea! It can happen. But it will take some radical people with radical love. Radical love. That's what your friends need. In this book you will find out how to have it and how to give it away. God wants to tap you on the shoulder, get you to look Him in the face, and challenge you to radically love your friends through the power of the Gospel.

You can make the difference at your school! Take the challenge to take your campus for Christ.

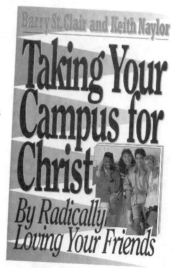

Building Leaders
For Jesus-Focused Youth Ministry

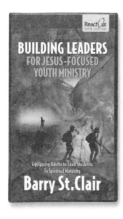 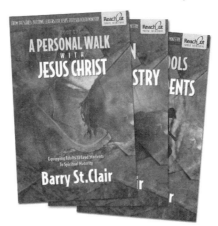

Barry St. Clair has created the tools you need for the leadership adventure. He designed them to build leaders in three areas:
- their personal relationship with Jesus Christ (book one)
- their vision for life and ministry (book two)
- their skills in working with students (book three)

Building Leaders for Jesus-Focused Youth Ministry offers youth leaders a biblical, practical plan to equip lay youth leaders and parents with the heart, vision, and skills to build relationships with and disciple believing students. It also trains youth leaders to relate to and communicate Christ to non-believing students.

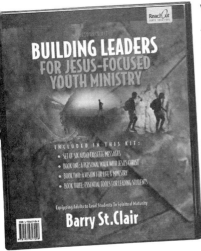

With the *Building Leaders For Jesus-Focused Youth Ministry Resource Kit* you will have three comprehensive, affordable, easy to use, interactive books and a series of audio messages. This three book set easily adapts to your church's calendar. Each book is designed for use over a twelve-week period of time that includes eleven sessions for discussion and one group experience.

For this and other books and resources:
Order online at www.reach-out.org
or by phone: 1-800-473-9456